TYLER FLORENCE /

STIRRING
THE POT

Meredith Books® / Des Moines, IA

Meredith Books
1716 Locust Street
Des Moines, Iowa 50309–3023
meredithbooks.com

Printed in the United States of America.

First Edition.
Library of Congress Control Number: 2008922214
ISBN: 978-0-696-24157-4

I would like to dedicate this book to New York City in honor of the 13 years that I spent in the greatest city in the world. Your people, your soul, and your life lessons have given me the backbone to truly be the best that I can be. I am eternally grateful. It was a hell of a ride and from the bottom of my heart, I thank you. —TF

STIRRING THE POT

HERE IT IS! EVERYTHING YOU NEED TO KNOW TO GET THE MOST OUT OF YOUR KITCHEN. TYLER FLORENCE BREAKS IT DOWN INTO CHAPTERS THAT ARE LOADED WITH SIMPLE TECHNIQUES, BASIC RECIPES, SOLUTIONS, AND TIPS TO HELP YOU FALL IN LOVE WITH YOUR KITCHEN ALL OVER AGAIN.

The vast majority of cookbooks on the market today deliver a lot of great recipes, but they can sometimes set you up for failure. It's like enrolling in a Masters Program but you're really looking for something on the 101 level. Cooking well is a progression, starting with the set-up of your work space to the selection of your ingredients to the time you actually apply the heat. If anywhere along the way you miss a step or try to cut too many corners, the end result will not be what you were looking for. From the set up of your kitchen to the contents of your refrigerator to your choice of cutlery, careful attention to the building blocks of great cooking will get you results in the kitchen. So let's start at the beginning with the very basics of the kitchen that every home chef should master. Learn how to organize and stock your fridge and pantry and take a peek inside for a list of Tyler's must-have kitchen equipment, tools, and gadgets. Once you have gone back to the basics (or maybe even acknowledged them for the first time), it's time to dive in. *Stirring the Pot* is full of tips, techniques, and recipes that everyone should master. In the spirit of keeping it simple, Tyler takes the guesswork out of cooking and dishes up a new book that will serve as the beginning, middle, and end of your everyday efforts to cook well and have fun doing it.

CONTENTS

PART 1: YOUR KITCHEN

PART 2: YOUR COOKING

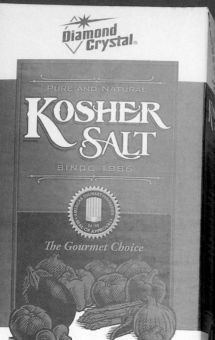

PART 1 / YOUR KITCHEN

organize / hardware

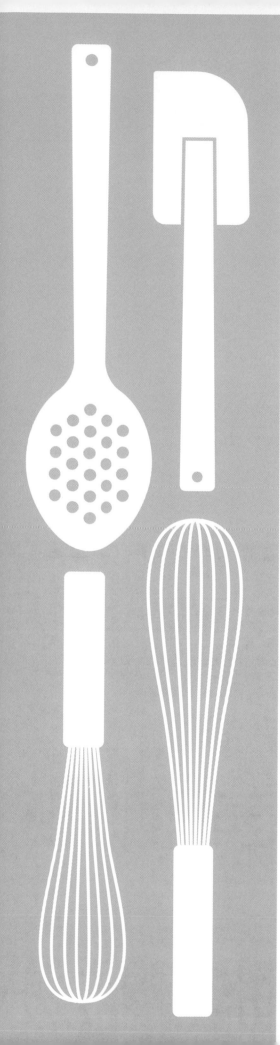
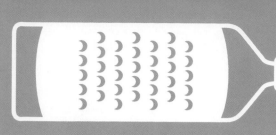
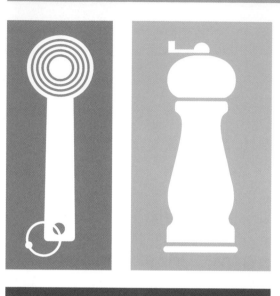

ORGANIZE

LISTEN, WE HAVE TO TALK. YOUR KITCHEN IS A MESS. I WOULDN'T SAY THIS IF WE WEREN'T FRIENDS, BUT YOU AND I NEED TO CLEAN HOUSE.

With a well-run kitchen, cooking can be a joy that you actually look forward to. First of all, you have to clean out everything that doesn't work for you anymore (including that broken toaster you can't fix). Pretend that you are moving out—that the 'old you' who collected and stored bits and pieces of everything is leaving town and taking the clutter along for the ride.

With the cupboards done, you are ready for my next point: counter space is everything. When you clean off your counters, you get your kitchen back. You can think clearly about the recipe you are working on. **CLEAN COUNTERS + A CLEAN KITCHEN = DELICIOUS FOOD.**

And here is something else I've learned over the years: When it comes to cooking, **ALL KITCHENS ARE THE SAME SIZE.** You can only chop mushrooms in a 3-inch space. A standing mixer only takes up 12 inches. A cutting board only takes up 24 inches. You can only stand and chop in 4 square feet. It's not the size of the kitchen you're working in, it's the way it is laid out. With that in mind, it's time to check out the pivot triangle …

ORGANIZE

the pivot triangle

OPERATING IN A WELL-DESIGNED KITCHEN IS A DANCE BETWEEN THREE POINTS. I CALL IT THE PIVOT TRIANGLE.

Walk into your kitchen and visualize a triangle between any prep space (POINT A), the stove (POINT B), and the fridge (POINT C). That is your pivot triangle—your cooking zone. It is as big as any space needs to be, and that is what we are going to organize, stock, and learn to efficiently utilize.

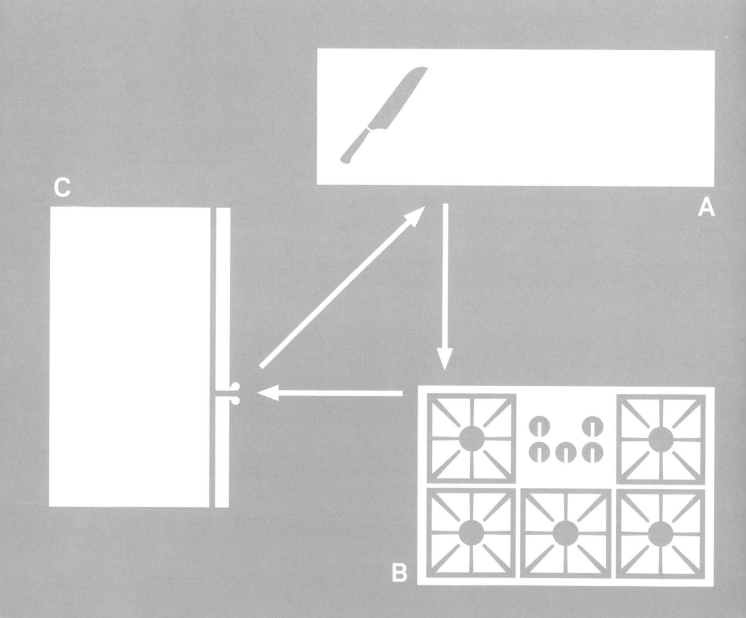

LET'S TALK ABOUT POINT A. Your prep space should have only a few key pieces on it. First and foremost, the cutting board, which needs to be big enough to really work on. A BIG CUTTING BOARD IS THE ANCHOR OF A GREAT KITCHEN. It's where you figure things out. Get a big beautiful wooden board that you will have for years. Next up, let's talk about where to put knives in your prep space. You need them within *your* arm's reach but not within the reach of your children. So that means up against the wall either in a knife block or on a wall-mounted magnetic strip. YOU ALSO NEED A PLACE FOR TOOLS in this prep space. Personally, I like the look of an oversize ceramic crock filled with wooden spoons, ladles, rubber mixing spatulas, tongs, and microplanes. Another option is to store everything in one of your newly cleaned-out drawers—as long as everything is within arm's reach. The final thing that you need in your prep space is a place for kitchen towels. GOOD KITCHEN TOWELS PROTECT YOUR HANDS. I like professional kitchen towels that are thick enough to protect my hands from the hot handle of a sauté pan or a baking dish just out of the oven. I keep my kitchen towels right on the counter, rolled tightly in an old French wine crate so they are easy to grab. With these great towels at hand, you can ditch your ratty old crocheted pot holders.

The seasoning station is a small tray set up with all your favorites—kosher or sea salt, a pepper mill, a bottle of good olive oil, and anything else that you use every day to season food.

LET'S MOVE ON TO POINT B IN OUR PIVOT TRIANGLE: the stove and oven—where all those exciting pyrotechnics happen. Here you sauté, sear, braise, caramelize, and make scrambled eggs for your kids on the weekends. Once the heat is on, you'll need to be able to think on your feet, SO HAVE EVERYTHING WITHIN ARM'S REACH. That means pots and pans are stacked up and separated neatly—big pots for pasta and chili in one cabinet, smaller pots for tomato sauce in the other. Now you are ready to roll. If you have some extra counter space to the left or the right of your stove, I would recommend a small, handy, easy-to-reach SATELLITE CROCK of wooden spoons and spatulas, as well as a SEASONING STATION. The seasoning station is a small tray set up with all your favorites—kosher or sea salt, a pepper mill, a bottle of good olive oil, and anything else that you use every day to season food. With all of these tools at your fingertips, you won't have to go looking for a pinch of salt when you're in the thick of it.

THE LAST PART OF THE PIVOT TRIANGLE IS POINT C: the refrigerator, freezer, and pantry zone of the kitchen. This is the most important of the three zones. If there is nothing in the fridge or pantry, you can't make dinner. It's that simple. So, let's take a look at them, one at a time, in detail …

YOU NEED TO BE ABLE TO THINK ON YOUR FEET, SO HAVE EVERYTHING WITHIN ARM'S REACH.

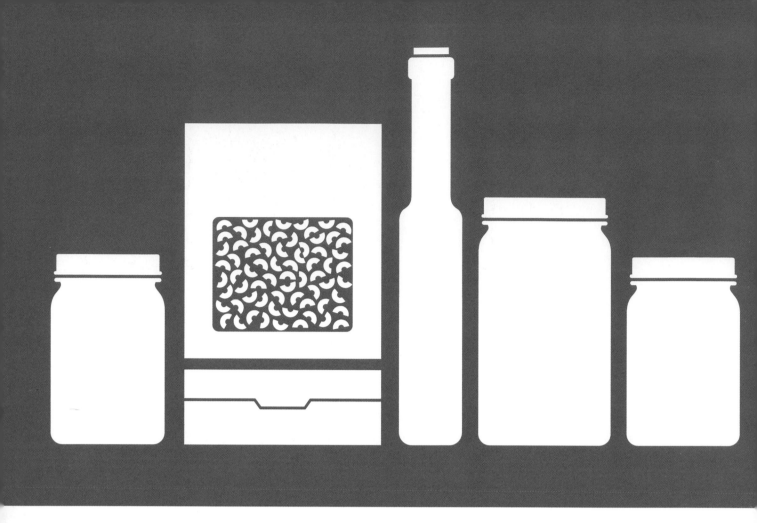

the pantry

LET'S TALK ABOUT THE PANTRY. I KNOW THAT IN MOST KITCHENS—INCLUDING MY OWN, ON OCCASION—THE PANTRY IS A GIANT BLACK HOLE WHERE THINGS GET PUSHED TO THE BACK AND OFTEN DON'T SEE THE LIGHT OF DAY FOR YEARS.

You have probably left yourself about 10 percent of the front shelf for new things. Bags of half-eaten cookies, stale potato chips, that hot sauce with your picture on the bottle that you received as a gift, it's all back there—but it's gotta go. The next step is to stake a position in the pantry for everything you need—pasta, canned goods, cereal, flour, olive oil, etc. This way, when you run out of something, there is an obvious hole and you know what you need to pick up at the market. And I know this sounds a little obsessive, but I like to turn the cans to face outward so I can read the labels and merchandise them like a grocery store. When I open an organized pantry, it immediately answers the question "what's for dinner?"

WHEN I
OPEN AN
ORGANIZED
PANTRY, IT
IMMEDIATELY
ANSWERS THE
QUESTION
"WHAT'S FOR
DINNER?"

IF YOU DON'T FOLLOW THESE RULES, YOU'LL SEE A FRIDGE FULL OF ODDS AND ENDS, BUT YOU WON'T SEE DINNER.

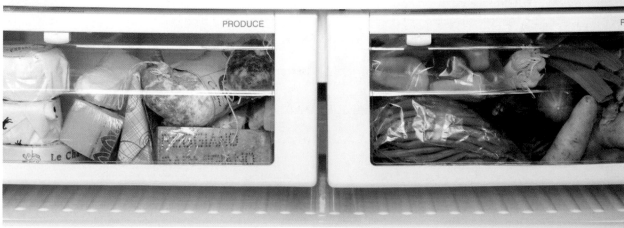

the fridge

NOW THAT WE HAVE THE PANTRY UNDER CONTROL, LET'S TALK ABOUT THE FRIDGE.

Repeat after me: FIRST IN—FIRST OUT, or FIFO for short. It's a simple rule of thumb to keep track of what's fresh in the fridge—what goes in first goes out first. Milk, butter, ketchup—use up the old stuff before you open the new stuff. And just like the pantry, if you're not sure when you bought it, chuck it. There is no reason to throw out perfectly good food, just don't be a pack rat. The idea is to have space for fresh food that you can actually cook with. Imagine replacing that half-eaten Danish box with fresh herbs and a pint of super-ripe cherry tomatoes that you can use for a quick pasta sauce. Refill that crisper drawer of wilted vegetables with leeks, celery, carrots, Yukon gold potatoes, and summer squash to have everything for an easy vegetable soup. All of a sudden you feel inspired, not frustrated, by what's in front of you. So go ahead—gut that fridge and get off on the right foot.

the freezer

NOW LET'S TALK ABOUT THE FREEZER. WHAT *IS* HALF OF THAT STUFF IN THERE? NAMELESS, FACELESS BUNDLES OF ALUMINUM FOIL CRUSTED IN FREEZER BURN …

How good could that possibly taste? Are you really going to defrost it and cook with it? Here's the deal: if you can't remember what it is, toss it out. After 30 days in freezing temperatures, steaks, vegetables, and everything else will begin to dehydrate. That crystallized moisture on the inside of the bag used to be inside your food. Your gorgeous and expensive New York Strip has now turned into frozen beef jerky. For me, your family, and yourself—throw it out. Only keep things in the freezer that you can actually use. A freezer can be a great resource when it comes to cooking because you can make recipes in volume and have dinner ready for another night. But, just as quickly, it can become a food graveyard. Let's take the time to really talk about what works in a freezer and what doesn't so that you can use it to your advantage …

MEAT All meat, for the most part, freezes the same way—pork, lamb, veal, beef, hamburger, you name it. And here's the deal: meat is very expensive so you can't just toss your beautiful pork chops into the freezer on the Styrofoam tray that they came on. You will ruin them if you do. If you are going to freeze meat, you need to treat it with respect. I always wrap meat three times to protect it from the elements—first a tight layer of plastic wrap, then a layer of foil, and finally a resealable freezer bag. Label the bag and/or the foil with the cut of meat, the number of portions, and the date it was frozen. And here's the most important part: put it in rotation and eat it. Try to only keep meat frozen for up to one week. After that, it really starts to deteriorate because of the higher fat content, which makes it a magnet for absorbing "off" odors in the freezer. Plus, when the tissue begins to constrict with the freezing air, it forces the natural moisture of the meat out to the surface where it turns into ice crystals. Before you know it, you have freezer burn on $100 worth of steaks. Remember, your freezer is not Siberia—don't banish food to the freezer, never to be seen again.

FISH A lot of people complain about how fish can taste "fishy" at times; I know what they mean. If fish has been frozen, you may get that "off" flavor. The oil in fish, such as tuna or salmon doesn't hold up well to the harsh environment of a freezer and can become pungent. I have never had luck with freezing fish, or shellfish for that matter. So, this is one where I advise you to only shoot for the freshest you can get your hands on. AVOID FREEZING FISH.

CHICKEN Whole chickens freeze really well, but they too have a tendency to absorb the odors in the fridge. So, again, I wrap them three times: once in plastic wrap to protect the flesh of the chicken, then in foil to stave off freezer burn, and finally in a large freezer bag to protect the flavor. It's the same principle with smaller bone-in pieces and boneless, skinless chicken breasts. The last thing is to put a proper label on the outside of the bag so you know what it is. Note the number of portions and the date you put it in the freezer. But please, only keep it in there for a month. Freeze anything longer than that and the quality really starts to deteriorate. (Remember, in our newly clean kitchen, we're thinking fresh!)

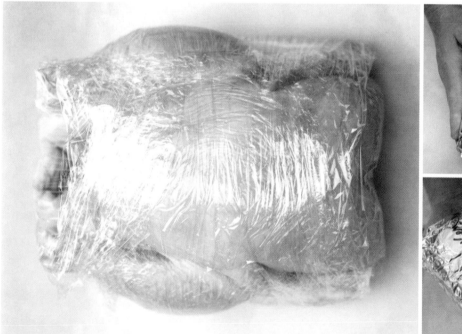

VEGETABLES Vegetables actually freeze quite well once they have been cooked—for example, zucchini slow cooked with garlic and Parmesan or baby eggplant cooked with miso, ginger, and sesame oil. Whatever cooked vegetable you want to save will freeze for up to a month in resealable freezer bags. The two reasons I prefer freezer bags are that I can force out as much air as possible and I can stack them flat on the shelves, which makes it easier to find and identify what I want in a freezer full of backups.

STOCK As a fundamental of cooking, a good stock is one ingredient I simply must have in order to prepare food. I make stocks about once a month and use them for everything: soups, risottos, deeply flavored braising liquids, mashed potatoes—I could go on and on. In fact, for all of the recipes in this book that call for broth, stock can be substituted for superior flavor. When freezing a batch, first the stock has to be completely cooled, then strained with a super-fine strainer. (A colander lined with a clean kitchen towel or several layers of cheesecloth will work in a pinch.) When it is strained and cooled, set up a small "filling" station with a stack of freezer bags. Label and date the bags with a permanent marker. (They are impossible to write on when they are filled with liquid.) Set a small to medium bowl on the counter with a towel under it (so it doesn't slide), then place a large plastic bag inside of the bowl and fold the opening of the bag back over the rim of the bowl. Carefully fill the bags about three-quarters full, leaving enough room to squeeze the air out as you seal them closed. Double-check the seal on the bag, then lay the bags flat in the freezer. In no time, you have the frozen building blocks of flavor that are infinitely better than anything you can buy.

REMEMBER, YOUR FREEZER IS NOT SIBERIA.

SAUCES When I cook at home, it's all about clean, market-fresh flavors and getting dinner on the table effortlessly. Pulling a homemade sauce out of the freezer can be a lifesaver, especially if family or friends pop by at the last minute. Like fresh stocks, sauces freeze very well. Use large resealable plastic bags—labeled and dated—filled three-quarters full. Force out the air as you seal them up and lay them flat in the freezer. The next time you forget that the folks are coming over for dinner, you have it covered.

THIS IS THE PERFECT RECIPE TO MAKE AHEAD AND FREEZE FOR LATER.

PASTA When kids get hungry, you only have a few minutes to put the fire out. That's why I like to freeze a few pasta dishes such as spaghetti with creamy tomato sauce or tubes with peas and bacon. The great thing about these healthy snacks is that you can control the portion, curb their hunger, and keep them from grazing on junk food all day—or at least until dinner is ready. Plus they can easily pop a bag in the microwave and feel self-sufficient. Cook the pasta, drain it in a colander, and run cool water over it so the pasta stops cooking. Coat the pasta with extra-virgin olive oil to keep it from sticking together when it gets heated up. About a cup of cooked pasta with ½ cup of pasta sauce makes a great snack that is hot and fresh after school. Add a label and date, and freeze (you know the drill by now).

BREAD A loaf of multigrain bread will last a long time in my house, so I usually toss it in the freezer to keep from having to toss it out. When I pull it out, I just pop two slices into the toaster and it's as fresh as the day it was baked.

My family also really loves my garlic bread—the perfect recipe to make ahead and freeze for later. When I'm at the market and find a good ciabatta or a crusty boule, I pick up a few. When I get home, I pull out the food processor and chuck in 15 cloves of garlic, a pound of butter, ¼ cup Parmigiano-Reggiano, half a bunch of fresh basil, a good pinch of sea salt, and a few cranks of black pepper. Then I give it a good buzz and out comes instant garlic-basil butter! I use a serrated knife to make deep slits into the bread crosswise—through to about the last inch (see photos, page 24). I butter the bread, stuffing the garlic-basil butter down into all the pockets. Finally, with a spatula, I smooth any leftover butter over the top of the bread. I tightly wrap my masterpiece in foil, stuff it in a freezer bag, label it, and freeze it for up to a month. (If the loaf is too big for the bag, I cut it in smaller pieces before wrapping it in foil). When I am ready to bake it, I put the bread into the oven at 325°F for 30 minutes. Now *that's* good eatin'!

SCRAPS Now if you want to be a pack rat about something, let's talk about how all of those trimmings left on your cutting board can save you a little bit of money. If you're making stocks, those little peelings of carrot, celery tops, mushroom stems, and garlic paper all have tons of flavor. At the restaurant, we burn through hundreds of pounds of carrots, celery, onions, and herbs every week. By separating all of the trimmings and scraps and saving them for later use, we save thousands of dollars per year, reduce our trash bill, and lessen the impact on our landfills. Label your scrap bags and freeze them—when you're ready, make some stock and count your pennies!

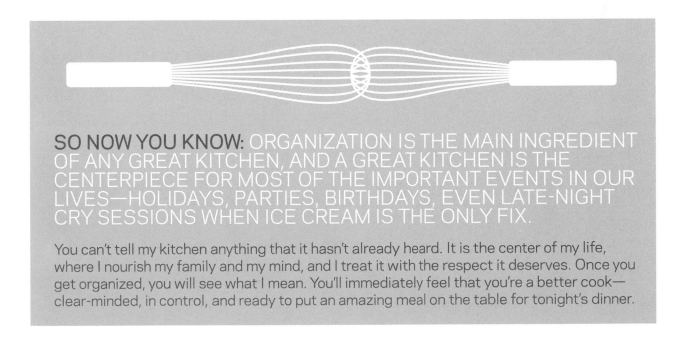

SO NOW YOU KNOW: ORGANIZATION IS THE MAIN INGREDIENT OF ANY GREAT KITCHEN, AND A GREAT KITCHEN IS THE CENTERPIECE FOR MOST OF THE IMPORTANT EVENTS IN OUR LIVES—HOLIDAYS, PARTIES, BIRTHDAYS, EVEN LATE-NIGHT CRY SESSIONS WHEN ICE CREAM IS THE ONLY FIX.

You can't tell my kitchen anything that it hasn't already heard. It is the center of my life, where I nourish my family and my mind, and I treat it with the respect it deserves. Once you get organized, you will see what I mean. You'll immediately feel that you're a better cook—clear-minded, in control, and ready to put an amazing meal on the table for tonight's dinner.

HARDWARE

GOOD EQUIPMENT GETS THE JOB DONE. YOUR KITCHEN DOESN'T HAVE TO BE LOADED WITH THE MOST EXPENSIVE COPPER SAUTÉ PANS OR THE NEWEST, HOTTEST KNIVES TO MAKE GREAT FOOD.

Your kitchen equipment has to give you great results, but how do you pick what will work? To narrow the field, I can recommend three lines of both cookware and cutlery that I have personally used. There are a lot of different knife makers in this world but only a handful of these knives belong in your kitchen. And to be honest here, we're going to have to go shopping. Don't worry, we won't break the bank, but we are going to find the best culinary investment for you.

cookware

AS MUCH AS COOKING IS AN ART FORM, A LOT OF SCIENCE GOES INTO THE MANUFACTURING OF THE COOKWARE WE USE EVERY DAY AT HOME.

When it comes to cookware, it is up to you to find your personal style, what looks right to you, and what feels good in your hand. You also need to look at thermal conductivity, the capacity of a material to conduct heat. Certain types of metals and just as importantly, the thickness of those metals, really make a world of difference in cooking. I'll tell you about three different brands of cookware that I use in my kitchens— three different constructions, three different looks, and three different price points. You'll find something here that will get you in the game.

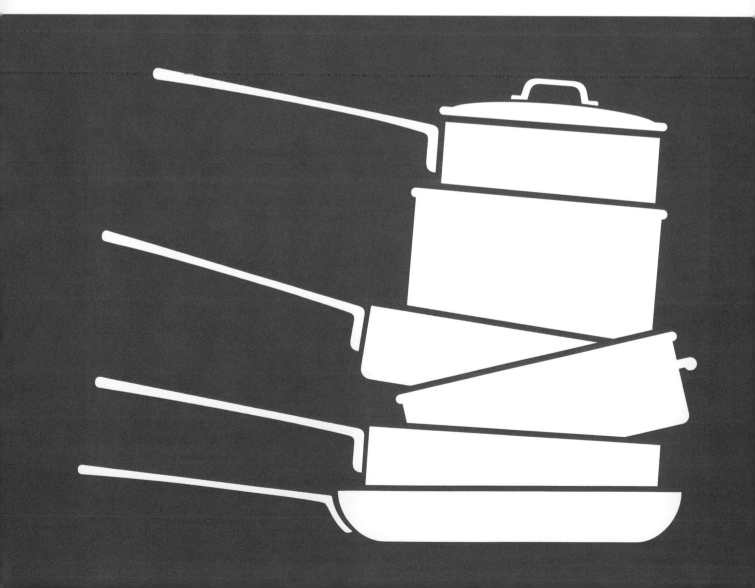

THIS HEAVY-DUTY COOKWARE LOOKS FANTASTIC AND WILL LAST YOU A LIFETIME.

FALK CULINAIRE COPPER COOKWARE I have always been drawn to the small, European family kitchens that look and feel like they have been filled with passionate cooks for generations.

On *Tyler's Ultimate*, I have brought this European feel to my kitchen with cookware from Falk Culinaire, a small, family-run company in Belgium. Decades ago, the craftsmen at Falk developed a technology for bonding a thin layer of stainless steel to a red copper vessel to create the ultimate combination of conductivity and thermal efficiency. Copper is a superior conductor of heat that allows your cookware to come to temperature quickly and evenly and is able to react quickly when you adjust the temperature on your stovetop. To top it off, this heavy-duty cookware looks fantastic and will last you a lifetime. That said, this stuff is about as expensive as it gets. But if you are willing to make the investment, you won't be disappointed.

ALL-CLAD METALCRAFTERS STAINLESS My 10-month old son, Hayden, loves shiny things. And let's face it, a little bling goes a long way with adults too. In all the years I have spent in kitchens, shiny stainless cookware seems to have been the "gold standard" for all kinds of cooks. It looks great, cooks great, and will never let you down. As a bonus, it is dishwasher-safe. When I use stainless steel cookware, I reach for the stainless collection from All-Clad Metalcrafters. All-Clad is an American company that began in the 1970s. They created a stainless collection that is "tri-ply" with three layers of bonded stainless steel construction, an 18/10 cooking surface that won't react with food, and a shiny, polished exterior. You will spend a few bucks on it, but you can start with a few pieces and work your way up until you have everything you need. It has a lifetime warranty, so you will never need to replace it.

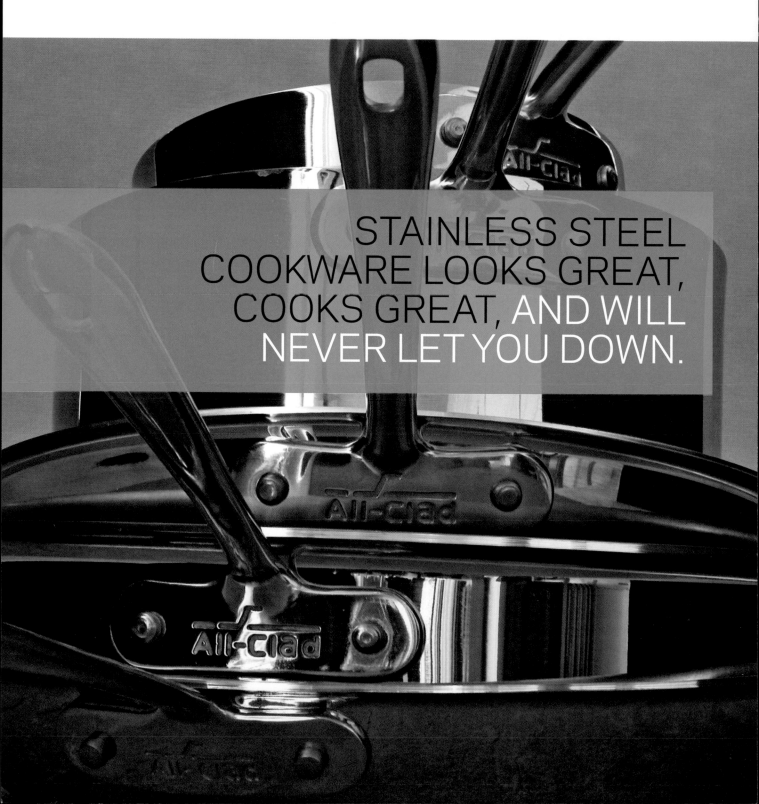

STAINLESS STEEL COOKWARE LOOKS GREAT, COOKS GREAT, AND WILL NEVER LET YOU DOWN.

FOOD TOOLS HARD ANODIZED COOKWARE Over the past 15 years, I have cooked with just about every type of cookware imaginable. Recently, however, an entirely new technology has come on the market that I have found to be superior in many ways—hard anodized aluminum. So for the past couple of years, I have been working to find the perfect combination of hard anodized aluminum and stainless steel for the ultimate cookware. All that hard work has finally paid off and I have created a cookware line that is both cutting edge and traditional in its approach to thermal conductivity, reactivity, and practicality.

Aluminum has long been regarded as a premium metal with excellent thermal conductivity and a resistance to corrosion and rust. Through a high-tech electrochemical process, aluminum becomes hard anodized, altering the properties of the metal and making it 2½ times stronger than stainless steel. I designed my line with a thick, hard anodized aluminum exterior from edge to edge to ensure even heat distribution throughout the entire body. I lined the cookware with polished 18/10 stainless steel for durability, reliability, and easy clean up. This line is also dishwasher-safe, something you won't usually find in hard-anodized cookware.

The Tyler Florence Food Tools Hard Anodized line is the best of both worlds (in my humble opinion). Innovative technology, gorgeous styling, and a reasonable price point make this new line a strong choice for your kitchen. If I didn't believe it, I wouldn't put my name on it.

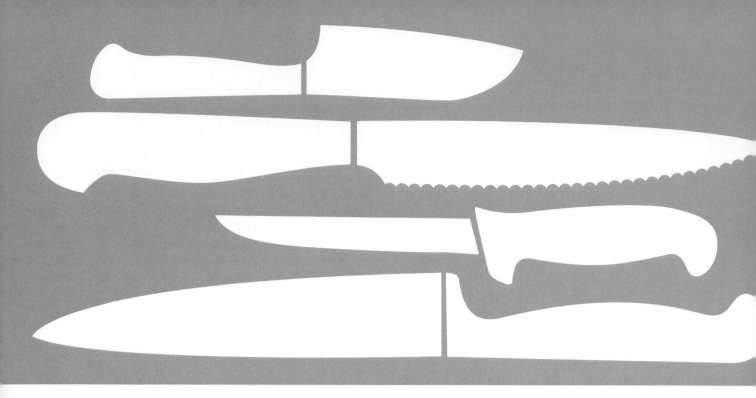

HARDWARE

knives

WHEN I FIRST STARTED COOKING IN THE LATE 1980S, THERE WERE ONLY A FEW PROFESSIONAL KNIFE BRANDS READILY AVAILABLE TO US—DEXTER-RUSSELL, VICTORINOX, HENCKELS, WÜSTHOF, AND F. DICK.

Knives have come a long way since I was a kid. Twenty years ago, they were either solid stainless steel, which didn't rust but couldn't hold an edge to save a life, or carbon steel, a metal that holds a very sharp edge but rusts like an old tin can and leaves a metallic taste on some foods. In response to these deficiencies, knife makers came up with high carbon stainless steel, an alloy that combines the best of both worlds. These knives can get razor-sharp like carbon steel and are stain-free like stainless steel. Most professional-grade knives nowadays are forged of this type of material, and this is the direction that I want to steer you. If you start here, you will find the perfect battle weapon to tell your chicken who's boss. And this time, it won't be the chicken.

Like your pots and pans, your knives are an essential part of your kitchen arsenal. Let's get your basic set together and learn how to keep your blades in proper shape so that you are set up for success when you get down to business. Knives are important—very important, in fact—and like your cookware, you will want to spend a little bit of money on them. I'm going to break it down for you with three suggestions of brands and styles to choose from. Get your collection started with any one of these three following lines and you are on your way.

FIND THE PERFECT BATTLE
WEAPON TO TELL YOUR
CHICKEN WHO'S BOSS.
AND THIS TIME, IT WON'T
BE THE CHICKEN.

THE JAPANESE STYLE OF KITCHEN KNIFE HAS A LOOK AND FEEL ALL ITS OWN

SHUN ELITE Growing up, I used to run around the house with my imaginary samurai sword, and although I still love wielding that sword, I am more likely to cross paths with an onion than a foreign army. The Japanese style of kitchen knife has a look and feel all its own and is worth considering for your kitchen.

The Shun Elite series of cutlery is directly inspired by the grandeur of the samurai sword, handcrafted in Seki City, Japan. Each knife has a smooth, rounded handle made of black PakkaWood, and these blades are as good as you're going to find, made with a core of exotic powdered steel that is purportedly much harder than most European knives (at 64 Rockwell versus the 56–58 Rockwell of most European knives). This super hard core is then clad with two layers of a softer stainless steel to provide strength, flexibility, and corrosion protection. With this combination of clad metals, the Shun Elite series achieves a sharp edge that keeps longer than most other knives. Because a lot goes into these Japanese works of art, you have to pay for it. But, like all of the equipment I recommend, these knives are meant to last a long time.

LamsonSharp™
Shelburne Falls, MA USA
Forged High-Carbon Stainless Steel
Silver
LamsonSharp™
Shelburne Falls, MA USA
Forged High-Carbon Stainless Steel
Silver
LamsonSharp™
Shelburne Falls, MA USA
Forged High-Carbon Stainless Steel
Silver
LamsonSharp™
Shelburne Falls, MA USA
Forged High-Carbon Stainless Steel
Silver

LAMSONSHARP SILVER Over the years, no matter what "hot" brands come and go, I have always found comfort and confidence in the granddaddy of American cutlery brands, LamsonSharp. Back in 1834 in Shelburne Falls, Massachusetts, Silas Lamson, the inventor of the curved scythe (that iconic tool of the Grim Reaper), opened up a factory to build his agricultural tools. A couple years later his sons, Ebenezer and Nathaniel, partnered with Abel Goodnow to start making knives in their father's factory. All these years later, Lamson & Goodnow is still putting out high-quality knives with one-piece, forged, full-tang blades. The beautiful oiled Rosewood handles are naturally durable and have a real weight to them that feels great in the hand. So if "Made in USA" is something that you are looking for in your product selections, go for the LamsonSharp Silver line of knives and you will make a solid investment. President Ulysses S. Grant was a fan of LamsonSharp and so am I.

WÜSTHOF CLASSIC IKON As I came up through the ranks in the culinary world, my knives were my best friends, always by my side. And like all of my peers, I was in a constant quest to have the best quiver of knives in the kitchen, both in quality and styling. For most of us, Wüsthof was the holy grail of cutlery and to many, that still holds true today.

Wüsthof is a German manufacturer that has been family owned and operated since 1814. Each knife is precision forged from a single blank of high carbon steel, tempered to 58 Rockwell and then triple riveted to the gorgeous black wooden handle. I love the Ikon Classic, the latest style from the company, as it has a newly designed handle that offers the ultimate in European styling with an excellent hand feel. I've come a long way since culinary school but I still consider Wüsthof one of the go-to brands in my kitchen. If you like the classics, take a look at Wüsthof for the ultimate in European craftsmanship.

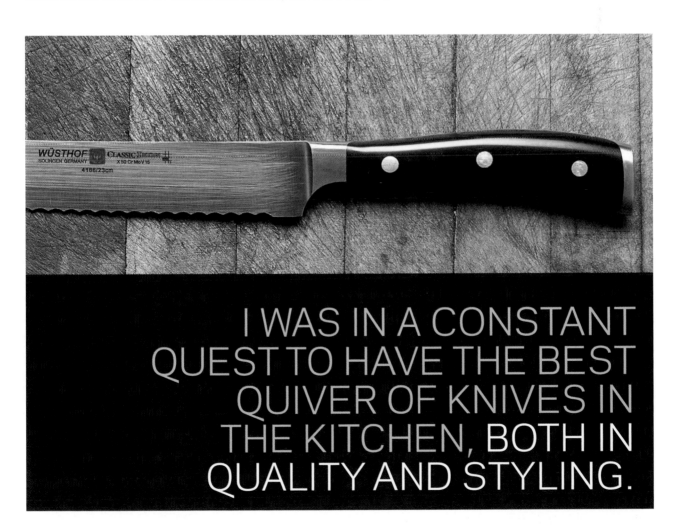

I WAS IN A CONSTANT QUEST TO HAVE THE BEST QUIVER OF KNIVES IN THE KITCHEN, BOTH IN QUALITY AND STYLING.

the right knife

THERE IS A DIFFERENT SHAPE AND SIZE OF BLADE FOR JUST ABOUT EVERYTHING YOU COULD EVER WANT TO SLICE INTO …

But you don't need all of them to get going. Most quality knife companies offer block sets that contain a variety of knives that will cover most bases. With a few extra slots in your block, you have the ability to add on as you find different shapes and sizes that you find useful or interesting. Let's identify some of the more popular and useful knives you will work with …

paring

santoku

chef's knife

cleaver

offset serrated

utility

bread

carving

boning

CHEF'S KNIFE Ranging from 6 to 12 inches, the all-purpose chef's knife will allow you to tackle just about anything. Pay attention to the size of the knife and pick the length that feels the most manageable in your hand.

SANTOKU KNIFE Also called a Japanese chef's knife, *santoku* literally translates to "three good things," referring to its three main specialties: slicing, dicing, and mincing. It has a wide, thin blade with an emphasis on balance but it is a bit shorter than a chef's knife. These knives often have a hollow ground edge to reduce friction as well. Do not use this knife for chopping through thick, hard materials such as bone.

BREAD KNIFE A long, serrated blade cuts through bread like a saw, working through the crust without applying too much pressure to the soft interior. The "teeth" of the blade allow you to cut by applying more horizontal pressure than a normal blade, where most cutting pressure is vertical.

OFFSET SERRATED This is the best choice for cutting through sandwiches as it has the serrated blade of a bread knife and will keep your knuckles above the cutting surface as you go all the way through the sandwich to the cutting board.

PARING KNIFE A short, straight knife of 3 to 5 inches with a sharp point, the paring knife is good in close quarters, with small ingredients, and for peeling fruits and vegetables.

UTILITY KNIFE Somewhere between the paring knife and the chef's knife in size, this is a go-to knife when working with small- to medium-size ingredients.

CARVING KNIFE This knife has a thin, long blade to slice turkey or other large pieces of meat.

CLEAVER This big, heavy, wide-body blade is used to chop through thicker and harder materials. Its weight and heft can crush through bone better than the chef's knife.

BONING KNIFE This short, thin blade, 5 or 6 inches long is used to deftly remove the bones within a cut of meat.

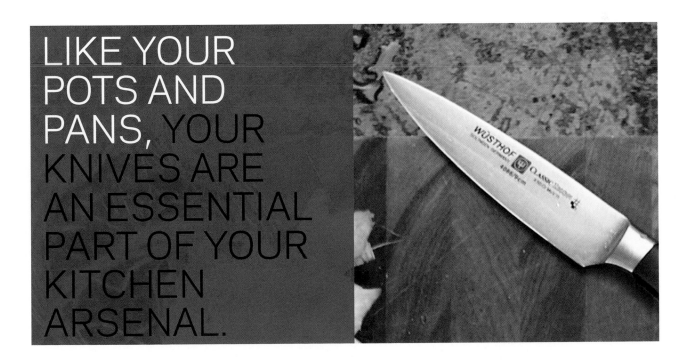

LIKE YOUR POTS AND PANS, YOUR KNIVES ARE AN ESSENTIAL PART OF YOUR KITCHEN ARSENAL.

sharpening

YOU CAN ALWAYS SPOT SEASONED COOKS BY CHECKING OUT THEIR KNIVES.

Not by how much the knives cost. Not by how fancy the knives are. But when a cook, home enthusiast, or professional has a quiver of well-cared-for blades that could split hairs, I can tell they're serious about their food. If your knife's blade isn't honed, using it is a lot more difficult and dangerous. Blasting through your prep work with a dull blade will slow you down and drastically increase the odds of dicing your finger instead of that red pepper.

    Each and every time I pick up a knife I start by feeling the blade's edge with my thumb. If it's even a little bit dull, I get out my whetstone. A whetstone is hands-down the best way to sharpen your knives. Some people might think that it's a complicated technique but it really isn't. Let's take it step by step …

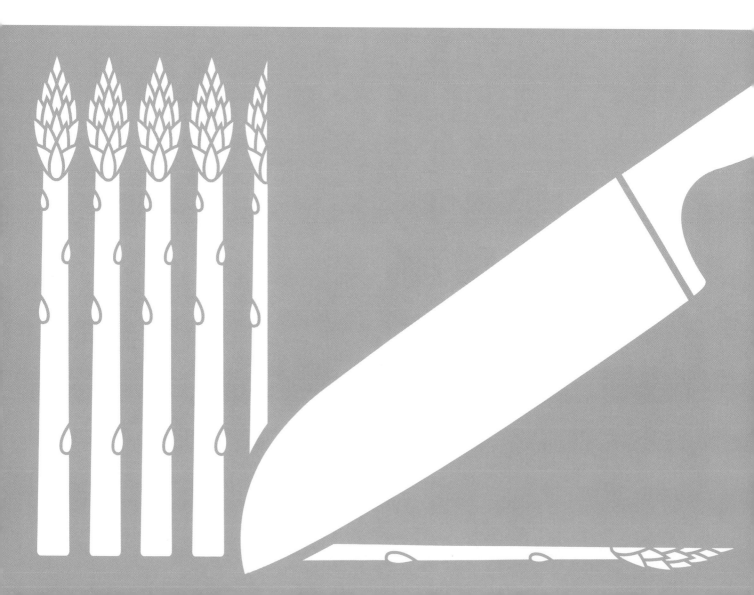

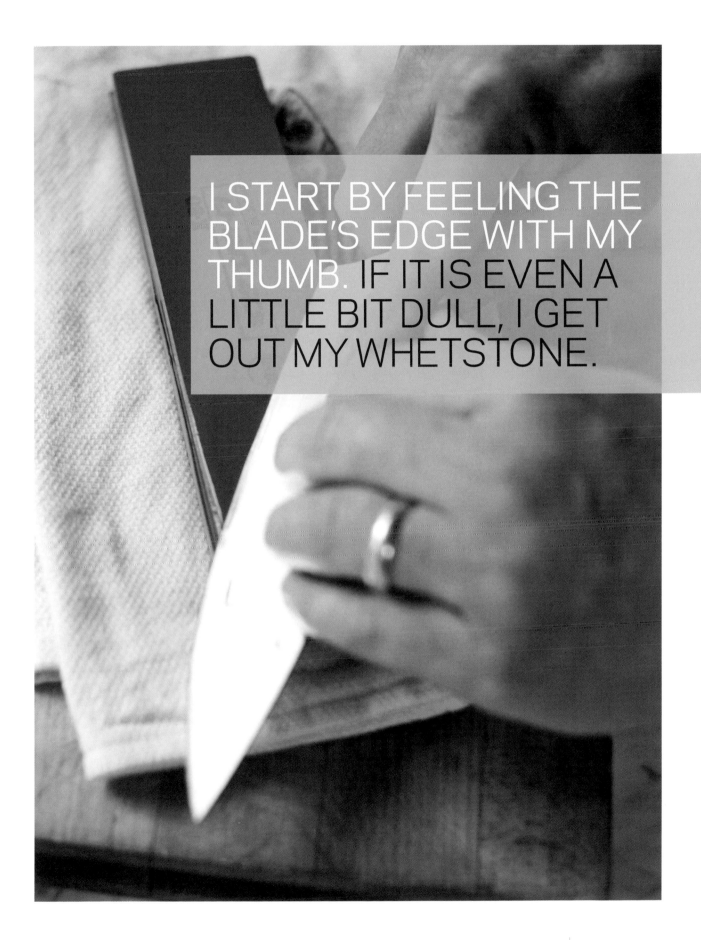

I START BY FEELING THE BLADE'S EDGE WITH MY THUMB. IF IT IS EVEN A LITTLE BIT DULL, I GET OUT MY WHETSTONE.

ONE Place your whetstone on a flat, stable surface. Lubricate the stone with either water or a light mineral oil per the stone's instructions.

TWO Place the knife handle in your hand with your index finger on top of the blade and your thumb on the spine. Place your other hand's fingers along the length of the blade and make sure the blade is facing away from you.

THREE Place the edge of the knife on the stone at an angle of about 20 to 25 degrees, about the same bevel as the edge of the knife.

FOUR Use your free hand, with fingers on the top of the blade, to apply even pressure to the back of the knife and carefully push the entire length of the knife over the stone, following the curve of the knife.

FIVE Turn the knife over and repeat the process. On this side, bring the knife toward you. Use the same angle, pressure, and follow the curve of the blade to bring the entire length over the stone.

SIX Repeat these passes over the stone until the blade is sharp. Make sure to always pass the same number of times on each side to keep your knife from coming out of balance.

SEVEN Wash, rinse, and dry your knife immediately.

Keep in mind that properly sharpening your knives is an art and may take some practice to get it down pat. If you aren't comfortable doing this yourself and you feel like your blades will live longer in the hands of a professional, by all means, find a local sharpening service to take care of them for you. Just make sure that whoever is doing the sharpening isn't using an electric grinder, as it takes too much metal off of your blades and ultimately ruins your knives and your investment. Now, with your razor-sharp blades at hand, you are ready for anything.

tools and gadgets

ON ANY GIVEN TRIP TO TYLER FLORENCE: MILL VALLEY, MY KITCHEN RETAIL SHOP, YOU WILL FIND SCORES OF NEW TOOLS, GADGETS, AND GIZMOS TO MAKE LIFE EASIER IN THE KITCHEN.

There are a lot of them out there and they are all useful in their own way. Here's a list of the most popular tools that you will want to throw in those crocks and drawers to have ready at hand. Check them off the list as you build your kitchen arsenal and continue to add to the list as your culinary repertoire expands.

Flat spatula	Measuring spoons	Electric rice steamer
Rubber spatula	Wine opener	Two 9-inch cake pans
Slotted fish spatula	Pastry brush	One 10-inch tart pan
Wooden spoon	Cutting boards	Cookie sheets
Slotted spoon	Kitchen towels	Muffin tin
Wire whisk	Kitchen string	Bamboo steamer
Balloon whisk	Wooden skewers	Food processor
Fine-mesh strainer	Mixing bowls	Immersion blender
Box grater	Chopsticks	Coffee grinder
Tongs	Pepper mill	Whetstone

PART 2 / YOUR COOKING

roast / sauté / braise / fry / grill / bake / steam / fresh and raw

COOKING

CONGRATULATIONS! IF YOU'VE MADE IT THIS FAR, YOUR KITCHEN IS A WHOLE NEW WONDERLAND.

Your pantry is orderly and packed with essentials. Your knives are sharp and your tools are readily at hand. We had a lot of work to do and you made it happen. Now let's get cooking!

When it comes down to it, cooking really isn't a scary process. For the most part, cooking simply refers to the application of heat to an ingredient. That heat can be applied in a myriad of ways and can produce a variety of results. Sometimes it's a wet heat (as in braising). Sometimes it's a dry heat (as in roasting). It can be direct or indirect. With fat or without. You get the picture. There are certainly variations and you will learn them as we go along. But for the most part, we really only need to focus on the seven major cooking techniques that make the world go 'round. I am going to hold your hand through the basics, step by step, so that you have each technique mastered and then I am going to give you some serious go-to recipes that you can keep in your back pocket for anytime crowd-pleasers. Here we go!

ROAST

HAVE YOU NOTICED THAT GIANT STEEL APPLIANCE ANCHORED TO YOUR KITCHEN WALL? WELL, THAT'S YOUR OVEN AND IT'S FOR ROASTING, NOT STORING POTS, PANS, AND OLD VCRS.

So clear it out, clean it up, and I promise you that together, we will fill your kitchen with warm, delicious smells and fantastic flavors. Way back when, roasting was done on a spit in front of a blazing fire. But over time, open flames indoors became less and less convenient, and roasting eventually found a home in our ovens. And while not quite as dramatic as an open fire, the oven can produce pretty darn close to the same effect. Simply put, roasting is surrounding a food with hot, dry air in an enclosed environment. When the heat hits the outside of the food, it reacts with the natural sugars and creates a gorgeous, savory crust of concentrated flavors on the outside and penetrates inside to cook the food all the way through. Repeat after me: **COLOR EQUALS FLAVOR**. Now, you'll want to adjust heat levels according to the shape and size of your meat or vegetables, but the principles remain the same.

When your food becomes caramelized and golden brown on the outside and hits the right temperature on the inside (use your thermometer!), you are almost there. I know that chicken is looking good, but do us both a favor—control your excitement and let the bird rest under some aluminum foil for at least 10 to 15 minutes. Roasting retains a lot of natural moisture, and cutting in too early will cause those beautiful juices to run out all over your cutting board. We don't want to lose a drop of flavor!

BACON-WRAPPED ROAST BEEF
WITH YORKSHIRE PUDDING AND GRAVY

serves 6 to 8 • time: 2 hours 30 minutes

"Them 'at eats t'most pudding gets t'most meat" is how the saying goes throughout the United Kingdom. A staple of the Sunday supper, this combination defines British comfort food. Traditionally, the pudding is used to catch the drippings of the beef and as a vessel for the gravy. And in this version, the addition of the bacon to the roast guarantees that both the tender beef and the hot pudding will be rich with flavor.

6   to 10 slices bacon
2   sprigs fresh rosemary, leaves only, chopped
4   sprigs fresh thyme, leaves only
2   garlic cloves, peeled and sliced
    Kosher salt and freshly ground black pepper
1   2-pound beef sirloin roast
    Extra-virgin olive oil
¼   cup all-purpose flour
1   cup reduced-sodium beef broth
1   recipe Yorkshire Pudding (see recipe, below)

Preheat oven to 375°F. Lay a sheet of parchment paper on a cutting board. Shingle the bacon slices on the paper. Sprinkle with rosemary, thyme, and garlic and season with salt and pepper. Lay the roast on the bacon and use the paper to help evenly roll the bacon up and around the roast. Tie with kitchen twine. Place the roast in a large roasting pan. Drizzle with oil. Roast about 1½ hours or until an instant-read meat thermometer reads 135°F for medium-rare when inserted into the thickest part. Allow the meat to rest for 25 minutes before slicing.

For the gravy, skim and discard the fat from the drippings in the pan, leaving ¼ cup fat remaining. Set the pan with the drippings and the ¼ cup fat over medium heat on the stovetop. Sprinkle flour onto drippings, stirring with a whisk until thickened. Whisk in the beef broth. Simmer about 12 minutes, until flour is completely cooked and gravy is slightly thickened. Season with salt and pepper. Serve sliced beef roast with Yorkshire Pudding and gravy.

YORKSHIRE PUDDING Preheat oven to 425°F. Grease a 9-inch round nonstick baking pan and place in the oven while you make the batter. For the batter, in a large bowl combine 1½ cups all-purpose flour, a pinch of kosher salt, 3 large eggs, 1½ cups milk (room temperature), and 2 tablespoons melted unsalted butter. Whisk for 2 to 3 minutes or until smooth and shiny. Pour batter into the hot pan and bake about 30 minutes, until pudding is puffed and golden. Serve immediately.

SALT-CRUSTED PORTERHOUSE

serves 2 to 4 • time: 50 minutes

Salt-roasting meat, fish, and even vegetables is a time-honored tradition. And while the abundance of salt might seem intimidating at first, don't worry, it's not going to end up in your food. When you crust your steak in the salt mixture, you are essentially creating a flavor seal and vapor lock—none of the good stuff is getting out. Your meat will roast perfectly.

- 2 18-ounce porterhouse steaks (1½ inches thick)
  Extra-virgin olive oil
  Freshly ground black pepper
- 6 egg whites
- 3 garlic cloves, peeled and minced
- 2 bay leaves
- 3 sprigs fresh rosemary, leaves only
- 4 sprigs fresh Italian flat-leaf parsley
- 3 sprigs fresh sage, leaves only
- 4 sprigs thyme, leaves only
- 3 cups kosher salt

Allow steaks to stand at room temperature for about 20 minutes. Drizzle with olive oil and season with a few turns of freshly ground pepper.

Preheat oven to 475°F. In a large bowl whisk egg whites until slightly foamy. In a food processor combine garlic, bay leaves, rosemary, parsley, sage, and thyme and pulse until finely chopped and combined. Add herb mixture to egg whites. Add salt and mix well until it holds together like a paste.

Place steaks in the center of a large cast-iron skillet or roasting dish and mound salt paste on top and around the sides of steaks. Roast about 15 minutes for medium-rare, until an instant-read meat thermometer registers 125°F when inserted into the center (temperature will rise when resting). Remove from oven and let stand for 7 to 8 minutes. Crack open salt shell; remove steaks, slice, and serve.

SLOW-ROASTED BEEF RIBS
WITH MUSHROOM STROGANOFF | serves 6 to 8 • time: 2 hours 45 minutes

This comfort classic has come a long way from its Russian roots and is a great example of how proper roasting can add an intense flavor to what can be a bland dish in the wrong hands. Great color and flavor on these ribs stand up beautifully to the creamy sauce and the flat noodles. "Low and slow" is the way to go with these ribs and you will find all of that hidden flavor.

3   pounds beef short ribs, cut into 2 ribs apiece
    Kosher salt and freshly ground black pepper
    Extra-virgin olive oil
2   cups sliced white button mushrooms
2   cloves garlic, peeled and minced
½   cup chopped shallots
¼   cup cognac
2   cups heavy whipping cream
1   tablespoon Dijon mustard
½   cup sour cream
1   pound egg noodles
3   tablespoons of unsalted butter
2   tablespoons chopped fresh Italian flat-leaf parsley
    Sprigs fresh Italian flat-leaf parsley, for garnish

Preheat oven to 300°F. Arrange short ribs on a roasting tray and drizzle with a little oil. Season well with salt and pepper. Roast ribs for 2½ hours until meat is falling off the bones.

Meanwhile, for the sauce, heat a large sauté pan over high heat and add a 3-count of olive oil (about 3 tablespoons). Add mushrooms and cook for 3 minutes, until brown. Add garlic and shallots and toss to combine. Season with salt and pepper. Cook for 2 minutes more, until garlic and onion become fragrant. Remove pan from heat and carefully add cognac, scraping to deglaze the pan. Return to heat and add whipping cream. Reduce heat and simmer, until reduced by half. Turn off heat and stir in mustard and sour cream. Season with salt and pepper. Keep warm until ready to serve.

Cook noodles in a large pot of salted boiling water according to package directions. Drain well; toss with butter and chopped parsley while still hot. Pile buttered parsley noodles high on a plate, top with ribs, and finish with stroganoff sauce. Garnish with parsley.

SLOW-ROASTED PORK SHOULDER WITH
SALSA VERDE AND GRAINY MUSTARD MASHED POTATOES | serves 6 to 8

• prep time: 4 hours *(includes marinating)* • cook time: 3 hours

1   4-pound boneless pork shoulder
2   tablespoons fennel seeds
4   garlic cloves, peeled
¼   cup chopped fresh rosemary leaves
¼   cup chopped fresh sage leaves
4   tablespoons kosher salt (1 tablespoon for every pound of meat)
1   tablespoon freshly ground black pepper
¼   cup extra-virgin olive oil
1   recipe Salsa Verde (see recipe, below)
1   recipe Grainy Mustard Mashed Potatoes (see recipe, below)
1   spring fresh Italian flat-leaf parsley, for garnish

Place the pork, fat side up, in a roasting pan fitted with a rack insert. For the rub, toast the fennel seeds in a small sauté pan over medium heat until fragrant. In a food processor combine the toasted fennel seeds, garlic, rosemary, sage, salt, and pepper. Pulse to combine. With the motor running, gradually pour the oil through the feed tube to form a paste. Rub the herb paste on the pork. Cover the pork with plastic wrap and marinate in the refrigerator for at least 3 hours or overnight.

Preheat oven to 325°F. Allow the meat to stand at room temperature for 30 minutes. Loosely cover pork with aluminum foil; roast about 3 hours, until juices run clear (160°F). Let the meat stand for about 15 minutes before slicing. Serve with Salsa Verde and Grainy Mustard Mashed Potatoes and garnish with parsley.

SALSA VERDE Soak ½ cup golden raisins in warm water until softened; drain. Rinse ½ cup salted button capers. In a food processor combine raisins; capers; ¼ cup finely chopped shallots; 1 cup fresh Italian flat-leaf parsley; the juice of 2 lemons; 1 tablespoon Dijon mustard; 1 teaspoon lemon zest; and ¾ cup extra-virgin olive oil. Pulse for 30 seconds, until combined. Season with kosher salt and freshly ground black pepper. Refrigerate for 30 minutes.

GRAINY MUSTARD MASHED POTATOES Heat 1 cup whipping cream and 4 tablespoons unsalted butter in a saucepan over medium heat until the butter melts; set aside and keep warm. Place 3 large peeled Yukon gold potatoes in a saucepan; add cold water to cover. Place saucepan over high heat; bring to boil. Add 1 teaspoon kosher salt; reduce heat. Simmer for 15 to 20 minutes, until the potatoes are tender. Drain. Pass potatoes through a food mill into a bowl. Stir in cream and butter mixture. Season with salt and freshly ground black pepper. Stir in a ¼ cup olive oil and 3 tablespoons whole-grain mustard.

BAKED FRESH HAM WITH
APPLE-CRANBERRY CHUTNEY | serves 8 to 10 • time: 2 hours 25 minutes

I am always surprised by how few people have enjoyed fresh ham this way and I can't wait for you to try it. Scoring of the fat allows the juices to flow right down into the meat, and when this beauty comes out of the oven, it will look like it's right out of the pages of a magazine. If you are looking for some sour-sweetness to balance the rich, hearty flavor of the ham, you will find plenty in this fresh apple-cranberry chutney.

1 5- to 6-pound fresh ham
   Extra-virgin olive oil
   Kosher salt and freshly ground black pepper

Apple-Cranberry Chutney
6 pink lady apples, halved and cored
2 cups cranberries
1 cinnamon stick
1 bay leaf
1 tablespoon pickling spice
1 tablespoon black mustard seeds
2 tablespoons sugar
1 1-inch piece ginger, peeled
1½ cups apple juice
½ cup apple cider vinegar

Preheat oven to 300°F. Put ham, fat side up, in a roasting pan and score fat. Rub with oil and season all over with plenty of salt and pepper. Cover loosely with foil and roast for 2 hours. Remove foil and roast, uncovered, about 1 more hour more, until an instant-read thermometer registers 155°F. Let the ham stand for 15 minutes before slicing.

While the ham is baking, combine the Apple-Cranberry Chutney ingredients in a large saucepan. Simmer for 25 minutes, until apples are almost falling apart and the sauce is fragrant. Remove cinnamon stick, bay leaf, and ginger; discard. Place apple mixture in a food processor; process until thick and smooth. Serve with baked ham.

MOVE OVER, HONEY-BAKED HAM: THIS FRESH HAM IS GOING TO BLOW YOU AWAY.

PAN-ROASTED PORK CHOPS WITH
CRISPY PROSCIUTTO AND ROASTED RED GRAPES

serves 4 • time: 1 hour

Adding a little fat to a pork chop is one of the best things you can do for "the other white meat." A mild, lean meat, pork really benefits from the extra flavor that this prosciutto adds. You can take it in any number of directions, but I think this classic Italian approach really works well.

2   quarts water
¼   cup sugar
¼   cup kosher salt, plus additional for seasoning
4   sprigs fresh thyme
2   whole cloves
6   allspice berries
4   bone-in pork chops, about 1½ inches thick
    Extra-virgin olive oil
1   pound California red grapes, on the vine and
        cut into 4 smaller bunches
    Freshly ground black pepper
8   slices (approximately 3 ounces) prosciutto
½   cup chicken broth
4   tablespoons unsalted butter, cut in slices and chilled
    Fresh Italian flat-leaf parsley leaves, for garnish

In a resealable bag combine the water, sugar, the ¼ cup salt, thyme, cloves, and allspice berries to make a brine. Add the pork chops, seal the bag, and refrigerate for 30 minutes.

Preheat oven to 425°F. Drain and pat dry pork chops. Set two large cast-iron skillets over medium-high heat and add a 2-count of olive oil (about 2 tablespoons) to each. Add 2 chops to each skillet and cook for 4 to 5 minutes, until golden. Turn chops, then push them to one side, and set grape clusters in pan. Drizzle with a little oil and season with salt and pepper. Place skillets in the preheated oven for 5 to 7 minutes, until chops are cooked through (160°F). Remove from oven and set chops and clusters of roasted grapes aside on a plate; keep warm. Place prosciutto on a roasting tray in a single layer and roast for 13 to 15 minutes, until golden and crispy.

Combine pan juices in one pan and set over medium heat. Add chicken broth to the pan, scraping the bottom to loosen all the brown bits. Whisk in chilled butter to thicken the sauce. Season with salt and pepper. Serve pork chops with roasted grapes, crispy prosciutto, and pan sauce. Garnish with parsley.

PERFECT ROAST CHICKEN | serves 4 • time: 2 hours 10 minutes

At Tyler Florence: Mill Valley, my kitchen retail shop, I have a constant loop of vintage shows of Julia Child's *The French Chef* playing on the wall. In my favorite episode, she roasts a chicken. Before she passed, Julia once mentioned that she was a fan of mine and I honestly couldn't have been more flattered. But she also said she didn't agree with my method of roasting a chicken, and I'll tell you, I've made it my mission to right that wrong. So I thought this would be the ideal opportunity to walk you through, step-by-step, roasting the perfect chicken. I think you will find this helpful and that it would make Julia proud.

1 4- to 5-pound whole free-range chicken
   Kosher salt and freshly ground black pepper
1 lemon, halved
1 garlic bulb, halved through the equator (horizontally)
1 sprig fresh rosemary
4 sprigs fresh thyme
2 sprigs fresh sage
¼ bunch fresh Italian flat-leaf parsley (about 4 sprigs)
2 sticks unsalted butter, room temperature
2 cups button mushrooms

Preheat oven to 400°F. Rinse the chicken with cool water, inside and out, and pat dry with paper towels. Season the cavity with salt and pepper, then stuff with lemon, garlic, rosemary, thyme, and sage. In a food processor combine the parsley and butter and process until well combined. Season the butter with salt and pepper.

Place the chicken, breast side up, in a roasting pan. Tie the legs of the chicken together with kitchen twine. Rub the herb butter over chicken. Put the mushrooms in the bottom of the pan; roast chicken and mushrooms for 1 hour 45 minutes, until the drumsticks move easily in their sockets and the juices run clear (180°F in the thickest part of the thigh). Baste the chicken with the drippings and rotate the pan every 30 minutes to ensure a crisp, golden skin. Remove the chicken to a platter, tent with foil, and let stand for 10 minutes before carving.

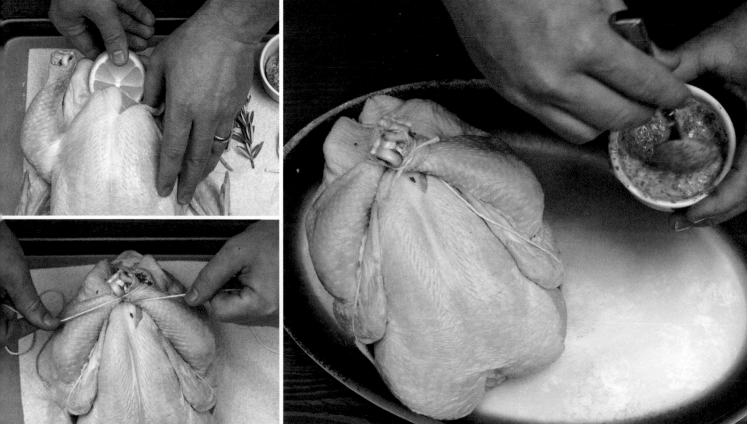

JULIA ONCE MENTIONED THAT SHE WAS A FAN OF MINE. BUT SHE ALSO SAID SHE DIDN'T AGREE WITH MY METHOD OF ROASTING A CHICKEN, AND I'LL TELL YOU, I'VE MADE IT MY MISSION TO RIGHT THAT WRONG.

POMEGRANATE-GLAZED
GAME HENS WITH CORNBREAD STUFFING

serves 4 • time: 1 hour 30 minutes

The Cornish game hen is the perfect single-serving bird, and this preparation is a must-do during the holidays. It is a sophisticated departure from that giant turkey you've been serving year after year—yet the holiday flavors are all still there. The beet mizuna and cornbread stuffing add a twist that nobody will expect but everybody will love.

Cornbread Stuffing

Extra-virgin olive oil
½ onion, diced
3 large cornbread muffins, crumbled
4 sprigs fresh sage, leaves only, chopped
1 egg
½ cup reduced-sodium chicken broth
Splash heavy whipping cream
Kosher salt and freshly ground black pepper

Pomegranate Glaze

2 cups pomegranate juice
1 tablespoon sugar
1 orange, quartered
1 sprig fresh rosemary
½ cup pomegranate seeds

4 1- to 1½-pound Cornish game hens
Kosher salt and freshly ground black pepper
½ stick unsalted butter, cut into 4 pieces
1 bunch beet mizuna or winter salad greens

For the Cornbread Stuffing, add a 2-count olive oil (about 2 tablespoons) to large sauté pan; caramelize onion over low heat for 8 to 10 minutes. Remove pan from heat; add crumbled muffins, sage, egg, chicken broth, and cream. Season with salt and pepper. Stir well to combine. Set aside

For the Pomegranate Glaze, In a small saucepan combine pomegranate juice, sugar, orange wedges, and rosemary sprig. Simmer over medium heat for 8 to 10 minutes until the liquid has reduced by half and glaze is rich and slightly syrupy. Add pomegranate seeds.

Preheat oven to 400°F. Rinse the hens with cool water, inside and out, and pat dry with paper towels. Season the cavities of the hens with salt and pepper and stuff with Cornbread Stuffing. Tie the legs of each hen together with a piece of kitchen twine. Season with salt and pepper, then put the hens in a single layer in a roasting dish. Top each with a piece of butter. Roast birds for 60 to 65 minutes, until the skin is golden brown and the juices run clear (160°F in the thickest part of the thigh). Using a pastry brush, baste the birds with Pomegranate Glaze every 20 minutes. Spoon pomegranate seeds from the sauce; use to garnish game hens. Serve with fresh beet mizuna.

ROASTED DUCK BREAST WITH APPLE-ONION PUREE

serves 2 to 4 • time: 45 minutes

Duck pairs beautifully with sweet fruit, and this combination is no exception. The acidity and sweetness of the apple stand up to the rich, meaty flavor of the duck, creating a great balance.

- 3 golden delicious apples, cored
- 2 duck breasts (about 1¼ pounds total)
  Kosher salt and freshly ground black pepper
  Extra-virgin olive oil
- ½ onion, sliced
- 4 sprigs fresh thyme, leaves only
- ½ stick unsalted butter
- ½ cup apple juice
- ¼ cup micro sprouts or other peppery greens, for garnish (optional)

Cut two to four ¼-inch-thick slices from one of the apples (1 slice for each serving) to roast. Peel and chop the remaining apples. Set aside.

Preheat oven to 400°F. Place the duck breasts, skin sides up, on a cutting board and score all over in a tiny crosshatch pattern so that the fat will render (melt out) and the skin will crisp. Season all over with salt and pepper. Lightly coat the bottom of a large sauté pan with a 2-count of oil (about 2 tablespoons) and place the pan over medium heat. When the oil is very hot, add the breasts, skin sides down, and cook about 8 minutes, basting with rendered fat, until the skin is brown and crispy. Place the duck breasts, skin sides up, and the apple slices on a roasting tray. Roast for 5 to 7 minutes for medium-rare (130 to 135°F in the thickest part of breast).

Meanwhile, in a large saucepan combine chopped apple, onion, thyme, and butter and place over medium heat. Add apple juice; cover and simmer for 12 to 15 minutes, until apples are soft. Puree in a food processor and season with salt and pepper.

Slice duck breast; serve over apple-onion puree with roasted apple slices. If you like, garnish with micro sprouts.

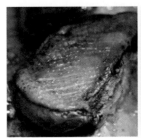  

SALMON "SLASHED AND STUFFED" WITH BASIL BUTTER

serves 8 to 10 • time: 45 minutes

While it was once a rare delicacy, salmon has become commonplace on the American table, and let's be honest, it can get a bit boring. So my friend Jerry Penacoli and I decided to spruce it up when we prepared this dish for the television show *Extra!* It was a hit! When you brush this basil butter right onto the fillet, you take it to a whole new level. Scoring the skin side not only gives you pockets for stuffing, it provides the perfect perforations for creating individual servings.

Ratatouille

Extra-virgin olive oil
3 garlic cloves, peeled and minced
Pinch crushed red pepper
4 sprigs fresh thyme
1 red sweet bell pepper, thinly sliced
1 large fennel bulb, thinly sliced
1 zucchini, thinly sliced into rounds
1 medium onion, sliced
2 cups cherry tomatoes
Kosher salt and freshly ground black pepper

Herbed Bread Crumbs

2 cups panko (Japanese bread crumbs)
1 bunch fresh basil sprigs (about 16 sprigs), leaves only
½ bunch fresh Italian flat-leaf parsley (8 sprigs), leaves only

Salmon

1 bunch fresh basil sprigs (16 sprigs), leaves only
2 sticks unsalted butter, room temperature
1 whole side of salmon, cleaned and scaled (about 2 pounds total)

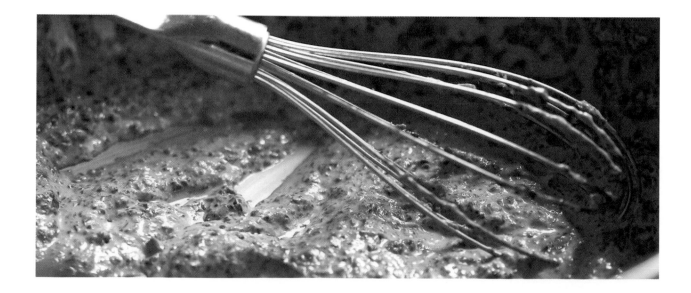

WHEN YOU BRUSH THAT
BASIL BUTTER RIGHT ONTO
THE FILLET, YOU TAKE IT TO
A WHOLE NEW LEVEL.

For the Ratatouille, place a large pan over medium heat and add a
3-count of oil (about 3 tablespoons). Add garlic, crushed red pepper,
thyme, and the vegetables, gently squeezing the tomatoes as you
add them. Season with salt and pepper. Sauté for 5 to 7 minutes until
vegetables wilt. Pour vegetables onto a sheet tray and set aside.

For the Herbed Bread Crumbs, in a food processor combine panko,
basil, and parsley. Pulse until crumbs are green. Set aside.

To make the Basil Butter, roughly chop the basil. In a food processor
combine basil and butter. Pulse until fully combined and creamy.

Preheat oven to 400°F. Using a chef's knife, make slits on the skin
side of the fish. Paint the skin side of the fish with the Basil Butter.
Carefully place the fish, skin side up, on top of the sheet tray covered
with Ratatouille. Bake about 15 minutes, until top is golden and
bubbly. Top the fish with Herbed Bread Crumbs and switch on the
broiler. Broil for 5 minutes, until golden and crispy.

GARLIC-AND-HERB-ROASTED
LOBSTER WITH CRISPY POTATO CHIPS serves 4 • time: 1 hour 15 minutes

This isn't exactly fish and chips, but it's certainly a decadent cousin. There is no need to deep-fry the rich, meaty lobster or leech its flavor by boiling it. Split it, roast it, and give it some beautiful color. The potato chips, wafer thin and extra crisp, are a fun and unexpected accompaniment to the luxurious crustacean.

½ bunch fresh Italian flat-leaf parsley
4 sprigs fresh thyme, leaves only
5 garlic cloves, peeled and gently smashed
½ stick unsalted butter, melted
   Kosher salt and freshly ground black pepper
2 cups panko (Japanese bread crumbs)
2 live lobsters (about 4 pounds total)
   Extra-virgin olive oil
2 lemons, cut into large wedges, to serve
   Drawn butter, to serve
1 recipe Crispy Potato Chips (see recipe, below)

Preheat oven to 400°F. In a food processor combine parsley, thyme, garlic, and melted butter and season with salt and pepper. Process until well combined. Add the panko; pulse 1 to 2 times just to combine. Set aside.

To kill the lobsters quickly*, sever the spinal cord with your chef's knife (use the tip of your knife to cut straight through between the head and tail). Using the tip of your knife, split and cut the lobster through the middle lengthwise. Discard the insides and the tomalley (the lobster's green-colored liver), and place the halves, cut sides up, in a roasting tray. Drizzle with oil, then pack on the panko crumb topping. Roast for 20 to 25 minutes, until the top is golden brown. Serve with fresh lemon wedges, drawn butter, and Crispy Potato Chips.

CRISPY POTATO CHIPS Fill a large heavy pot with 3 to 4 inches of vegetable oil. Heat oil to 375°F. Meanwhile, peel 2 new potatoes. Thinly slice the potatoes using a mandoline or a sharp knife. Drop potato slices in a bowl of ice water to remove excess starch; drain and squeeze dry in a kitchen towel. Fry potatoes in small batches for 2 to 3 minutes, until golden brown and crispy. Remove chips with a slotted spoon. Quickly drain chips on paper towels, then season chips with sea salt while still hot (so the salt sticks).

*NOTE You can also have your fishmonger kill the lobsters before you take them home.

ROASTED ACORN SQUASH
STUFFED WITH CHEESE TORTELLINI

serves 4 • time: 50 minutes

Acorn squash is available all winter long, when many vegetables are scarce, and is perfect for roasting. What I love about the acorn squash is that when you cut it in half, you have a beautifully delicious vessel for serving another meal component. These cheese tortellini are relatively rich, so a little goes a long way, and they fit perfectly in a squash half.

- 2 medium acorn squash (about 1 pound each)
   Kosher salt and freshly ground black pepper
   Extra-virgin olive oil
- 1 pound store-bought fresh or frozen cheese tortellini
- 2 cups heavy whipping cream
- 1 garlic clove, peeled and crushed
- 1 sprig fresh thyme, leaves only
- 1 cup grated Parmigiano-Reggiano, plus more for topping
- ⅛ teaspoon freshly grated nutmeg
   Fresh sage leaves, for garnish

Preheat oven to 350°F. Cut the squash in half through the equator and scrape out the seeds with a spoon. Cut a small piece off the rounded edge of both halves to give them a base to sit on. Place the squash halves, cut sides up, on a baking sheet and sprinkle with salt and pepper. Drizzle with oil and roast for 25 to 30 minutes until tender.

Cook the tortellini in salted boiling water according to package directions; drain well, reserving some of the pasta water. Set tortellini and pasta water aside.

In a separate saucepan heat the cream over medium heat. Add garlic and thyme; cook 5 to 7 minutes, until liquid is reduced and mixture coats the back of a wooden spoon. Add the 1 cup the Parmigiano-Reggiano and the nutmeg, stir over low heat to melt the cheese. Toss tortellini into cream mixture. (Use some of the pasta water to thin sauce, if necessary.) Season with salt and pepper, then divide among cooked squash bowls.

Turn the oven to 400°F. Sprinkle the tops with Parmigiano-Reggiano and fresh sage leaves; bake for 10 minutes more, until the cheese is melted and golden.

ROASTED TOMATO SOUP WITH FRESH BASIL

serves 4 to 6 • time: 1 hour

Roasting changes the properties of food, and this simple soup is a great example of that. When roasted, the flavor of tomatoes becomes concentrated and much more smoky than in fresh tomatoes. The basil comes through nicely as a sweet and familiar match.

2½ pounds fresh tomatoes (mix of heirlooms, cherry, vine, and plum tomatoes)
2 small yellow onions, sliced
6 garlic cloves, peeled
Cherry tomatoes, on the vine, for garnish (optional)
½ cup extra-virgin olive oil
Kosher salt and freshly ground black pepper
4 cups chicken broth
2 bay leaves
4 tablespoons unsalted butter
½ cup chopped fresh basil leaves
¾ cup heavy whipping cream
1 cup croutons (optional)

Preheat oven to 450°F. Wash, core, and cut the tomatoes into halves. Spread the tomatoes, onions, and garlic onto a baking tray. (Add the cherry tomatoes, if using for garnish, leaving them whole and on the vine). Drizzle with the olive oil and season with salt and pepper. Roast for 20 to 30 minutes, until caramelized.

Remove cherry tomatoes on the vine and set aside for later use as a garnish. Transfer the remaining roasted tomatoes and the onions and garlic to a large stockpot. Pour in any roasting liquid from the tray, about 3 cups of the chicken broth, the bay leaves, and butter. Bring to a boil, reduce heat, and simmer for 15 to 20 minutes, until liquid has reduced by a third.

Remove and discard bay leaves. Add chopped basil leaves. Puree the soup with an immersion blender* until smooth. Return soup to low heat; add the ¾ cup cream and adjust consistency with remaining chicken broth, if necessary. Season to taste with salt and pepper. Ladle soup into bowls. If you like, garnish each bowl with roasted cherry tomatoes and/or croutons.

*NOTE If you do not own an immersion blender, you can puree soup in a regular blender in small batches. Add a small amount of soup to the blender, then hold the lid down tightly with a kitchen towel over the lid while blending. Be very careful; the steam can cause the lid to shoot off and the hot soup can burn you.

SAUTÉ

OKAY, I KNOW THAT YOU ARE EXCITED ABOUT THAT BIG NEW TOY IN YOUR KITCHEN—THE OVEN—AND YOU CAN'T WAIT TO GET STARTED. BUT, WAIT, THERE'S MORE.

Let's move to your stovetop. Now you are most likely looking at anywhere from two to four burners, probably gas or electric, and you feel like you've been here before. You have flipped a grilled cheese sandwich in your time, and you can boil pasta of all shapes and sizes. But in these next few chapters, I am going to make this stovetop your new best friend. Sautéing (aka pan frying) is one of the most interactive and satisfying moves in your repertoire. Let's talk about what we are really looking for in a sauté.

Sautéing involves cooking food in direct contact with a hot pan and a little bit of hot fat. The moisture that comes out of the heated food evaporates immediately and caramelizes on the outside. Like with roasting, we are aiming for that savory brown crust on the outside of our food. Remember: **COLOR STILL EQUALS FLAVOR.** But in order to get that browning, we need to consider time and space. If you are trying to get a crust on a pork chop, give it time and don't overcrowd the pan. If you keep flipping it over and over, you're not allowing the crust to form and you won't get the flavor and texture you want. If you overcrowd the pan, you will end up boiling or steaming your food, as the temperature will drop and there will be too much moisture to evaporate instantly. Follow me as I walk you through the basics of sautéing to create some of the most deliciously satisfying meals you have ever had …

CHICKEN PARMESAN | serves 4 • time: 1 hour 5 minutes

Classics are classics for a reason, and this recipe is my take on a fixture of Italian cuisine. Named for its origins in Parma, Italy (not the type of cheese used), this dish really deserves the sauté treatment to get the most flavor on the outside of your chicken. Fresh mozzarella goes a long way here too—once you try it, you'll stick with it.

	Extra-virgin olive oil
1	medium onion, chopped
2	garlic cloves, peeled and minced
2	bay leaves
½	bunch fresh basil sprigs (about 8 sprigs), leaves only
½	cup kalamata olives, pitted
2	28-ounce cans whole San Marzano tomatoes, drained and hand-crushed
	Pinch sugar
	Kosher salt and freshly ground black pepper
4	skinless, boneless chicken breast halves (about 1½ pounds total)
½	cup all-purpose flour
2	large eggs, lightly beaten
1	tablespoon water
1	cup dried bread crumbs
1	8-ounce ball fresh buffalo mozzarella, drained
	Freshly grated Parmigiano-Reggiano
1	pound spaghetti

In a large sauté pan heat a 2-count of oil (about 2 tablespoons) over medium heat. When the oil is hot and hazy, add the onion, garlic, and bay leaves; cook and stir for 5 minutes until fragrant and soft. Hand tear half of the basil leaves. Add the olives and hand-torn basil. Carefully add the tomatoes; cook and stir about 15 minutes until the liquid is cooked down and the sauce is thick. Season with sugar, salt, and pepper. Lower the heat, cover, and keep warm.

Preheat oven to 450°F. Set chicken breasts on a cutting board and cover with plastic wrap. Pound the chicken breasts with the flat side of a meat mallet until they are about ½ inch thick. Put the flour on a large shallow plate; season flour with salt and pepper. Combine the eggs and water in a wide bowl and beat until frothy. Put the bread crumbs on another large plate and season with salt and pepper.

In a large ovenproof sauté pan heat a 3-count of oil (about 3 tablespoons) over medium-high heat. Lightly dredge both sides of the chicken cutlets in the seasoned flour, then dip them in the egg wash to coat completely, letting the excess drip off. Finally,

dredge the cutlets in the bread crumbs. When the oil in the skillet is hot, add the cutlets and sauté for 4 minutes on each side, until golden and crusty, turning once.

Set aside 1 cup of the tomato-olive sauce. Pour the remaining sauce over the chicken and sprinkle with mozzarella and Parmigiano-Reggiano. Bake about 15 minutes or until cheese is bubbly.

Meanwhile, cook spaghetti in a large pot of boiling salted water according to package directions; drain. Toss spaghetti with reserved tomato-olive sauce. Cut the remaining basil leaves into shreds. Serve chicken with spaghetti. Garnish with shredded basil.

SWEET MARSALA WINE AND FRESH MUSHROOMS ARE A RICH AND SATISFYING COMBINATION THAT NEVER GOES OUT OF STYLE.

CHICKEN WITH
MUSHROOMS AND MARSALA

serves 4 • time: 1 hour 5 minutes

You have enjoyed this dish time and again at your favorite Italian restaurant and now you can make it at home. The sweet Marsala wine and fresh mushrooms are a rich and satisfying combination that never goes out of style.

1	3-pound whole free-range chicken, cut into 8 pieces
	Kosher salt and freshly ground black pepper
	Extra-virgin olive oil
½	stick unsalted butter, room temperature
2	garlic cloves, peeled and minced
½	bunch fresh thyme sprigs (about 8 sprigs)
2	cups button mushrooms, halved
2	shallots, diced
1½	cups sweet Marsala wine
1	cup chicken broth
½	stick unsalted butter, cut into cubes
2	cups penne pasta

Rinse the chicken pieces with cool water, then pat dry with paper towels. Season the chicken pieces well with salt and pepper.

In a large roasting pan heat a 3-count of olive oil (about 3 tablespoons) over medium heat. Add chicken and brown in hot oil about 10 minutes, until golden all over, turning pieces occasionally to brown on both sides. Remove chicken from pan and set aside on a plate tented with aluminum foil. Add garlic, thyme, mushrooms, and shallots to hot roasting pan. Season with salt and pepper and sauté until mushrooms are brown and shallots are slightly caramelized. Deglaze the pan with Marsala and chicken broth, scraping the brown bits off the bottom of the pan with a wooden spoon.

Nestle the chicken back in the pan, making sure each piece has good contact with the bottom of the pan. Top each chicken piece with butter. Cover the pan, leaving lid slightly askew. Cook over medium-low heat for 30 minutes until chicken is cooked through (180°F), basting the chicken with the pan juices periodically.

Meanwhile, in a large pot of boiling salted water, cook penne pasta according to package directions; drain. Season the chicken with salt and pepper. Serve with hot penne.

CHICKEN BREAST WITH
ORANGE, OLIVES, AND NEW POTATOES

serves 2 to 4 • time: 45 minutes

Leave the skin on the chicken breasts and give it a gorgeous pan-sear that will create a delicious, savory crust. The olives lend this dish Mediterranean flare and the orange is a refreshing and unexpected burst of flavor.

	Extra-virgin olive oil
2	large chicken breast halves, skin on
	Kosher salt and freshly ground black pepper
4	new potatoes, sliced ¼ inch thick
1	cup black olives, pitted
½	orange, sliced
	Fresh Italian flat-leaf parsley leaves, for garnish

Preheat oven to 350°F. In a large ovenproof sauté pan heat a 3-count of olive oil (about 3 tablespoons) over medium heat. Season chicken breasts with salt and pepper; add them to the pan, skin sides down. Cook for 10 minutes until the skin is golden brown, then turn breasts over and add potatoes, olives, and orange slices. Cook for 5 minutes more, until the potatoes begin to brown. Season with salt and pepper. Transfer pan to oven and bake for 12 to 15 minutes, until chicken is golden brown and juices run clear (180°F). Garnish with fresh parsley leaves.

SAUTÉING IS ONE OF THE MOST INTERACTIVE AND SATISFYING MOVES IN YOUR REPERTOIRE.

CALIFORNIA BACON AND EGGS | serves 4 • time: 1 hour

This is one of the first dishes I came up with when I moved out West, and I find myself preparing it over and over again. I have served it for breakfast and I have served it at a black-tie evening gala at the Palace Hotel in San Francisco. Somehow, it seems to work just about anytime, anyplace. The eggs are local and fresh, the potato pancake is crispy and savory, and the bacon is smoky and delicious. But what really sends this one beyond breakfast is the delicate fresh celery pesto.

Crispy Potato Pancakes
4 medium Yukon gold potatoes
¼ cup finely diced onion
2 egg whites
3 tablespoons rice flour
Kosher salt and freshly ground black pepper
Extra-virgin olive oil

6 slices bacon
2 tablespoons extra-virgin olive oil
4 eggs

Celery Pesto
2 celery ribs, peeled
½ cup celery leaves
½ cup fresh Italian flat-leaf parsley leaves
1 garlic clove, peeled and smashed
¼ cup toasted walnuts
¼ cup extra-virgin olive oil
2 tablespoons grated Parmigiano-Reggiano
Kosher salt and freshly ground black pepper
Celery leaves, for garnish

To prepare Crispy Potato Pancakes, peel and shred potatoes using a mandoline or grater. Place shreds in a kitchen towel and squeeze out any moisture. In a large bowl combine potato, onion, egg whites, and rice flour. Mix well and season with salt and pepper. In a large nonstick skillet heat a 3-count of oil (about 3 tablespoons) over medium-high heat. Add spoonfuls of the potato mixture to make free-form cakes about 4 inches in diameter. Fry until golden brown, turning once. Drain on paper towels and season with salt and pepper. Keep warm.

In a sauté pan fry bacon over medium-high heat, stirring as it cooks so it curls up. Drain and set aside on paper towels.

In large nonstick skillet heat the 2 tablespoons oil over medium heat. Gently add the eggs and fry, sunny-side up, until the yolks are cooked but still runny in the centers. Keep warm.

Just before serving, prepare the Celery Pesto. In a blender combine celery ribs, the ½ cup celery leaves, the parsley, garlic, walnuts, and the ¼ cup olive oil and process until well combined. Add Parmesan and adjust seasoning with salt and pepper.

To assemble, place a spoonful of Celery Pesto on each plate. Top with a Crispy Potato Pancake and a fried egg, sunny-side up. Season with a little salt and pepper. Top with bacon and garnish with celery leaves.

VEAL PICCATA WITH LEMON, CAPERS, AND PARSLEY-BUTTER SAUCE

serves 4 • time: 40 minutes

Veal is a delicate meat that benefits from some extra fat in the pan as you brown the meat and seal in the natural juices. Some people find veal on the bland side, but you'll have no shortage of flavor when you serve this old-school combination of lemon, capers, parsley, and butter. Veal Piccata is an Italian classic that never goes out of style, and is a great dish to prepare at home.

1	pound spaghetti
	Extra-virgin olive oil
½	cup all-purpose flour
	Kosher salt and freshly ground black pepper
4	8-ounce veal cutlets
2	eggs
1	tablespoon water
1	cup dry white wine
1	lemon, juice only
2	tablespoons capers, washed and drained
1	tablespoon chopped fresh Italian flat-leaf parsley
½	stick unsalted butter, chilled and cut into cubes
	Italian flat-leaf parsley leaves, for garnish

Bring a large stockpot of salted water to a boil. Add spaghetti and cook according to package directions. Drain and set aside.

Meanwhile, in a large sauté pan heat a 3-count of olive oil (about 3 tablespoons) over medium heat. Season flour with salt and pepper; dredge cutlets in flour to coat. Beat eggs and water in a bowl; season with salt and pepper. Dip cutlets in egg wash, then place in the hot sauté pan. Cook veal about 2 minutes per side, until golden brown. Remove veal to a plate. Deglaze pan with wine, scraping up brown bits with a wooden spoon. Cook wine until reduced by half. Stir in lemon juice, capers, and the 1 tablespoon parsley. Gradually add the cold butter cubes whisking to thicken the sauce. Season to taste.

Serve veal over pasta and top with capers and parsley butter sauce. Garnish with parsley leaves.

CALF'S LIVER WITH
PANCETTA, SAGE, AND MASHED POTATOES | serves 4 • time: 45 minutes

I know, I know, you hate liver! Well, if you can tell me the last time you actually had it, I'll let you slide. But since you probably can't remember, give this recipe a try and I think you'll change your mind. Calf's liver is very tender and rich with a unique texture that is hard to beat. While it may not be diet food, it is very high in protein and nutrients. And because it is very rich, a little goes a long way. C'mon, trust me; give calf's liver another shot.

Extra-virgin olive oil
½ bunch fresh sage sprigs (about 8 sprigs), leaves only
8 slices pancetta, thinly sliced
1 pound calf's liver, sliced into 4 thin pieces
Kosher salt and freshly ground black pepper
½ cup beef broth
½ stick cold unsalted butter, cut into cubes
1 recipe Velvety Mashed Potatoes (see recipe, page 111)

Add a 3-count of olive oil (about 3 tablespoons) to a small saucepan and heat over medium-low heat. Fry sage leaves for 2 to 3 minutes until crispy. Remove with a slotted spoon and drain on paper towels. Set aside.

In a large sauté pan heat a 3-count of olive oil (about 3 tablespoons) over medium heat. Fry pancetta until crispy and fat has rendered. Remove pancetta and place on a paper towel to drain. Return pan to heat, reserving the fat in the pan. Season calf's liver with salt and pepper. When pan is very hot, add calf's liver and cook for 35 to 40 seconds per side so it is still pink in the middle. Remove calf's liver; set aside. Deglaze pan with the broth, scraping the brown bits off the bottom of the pan with a wooden spoon. Simmer and reduce for 3 to 4 minutes until darker in color and flavor is concentrated. Gradually add butter, constantly whisking, to thicken and add a glossy finish to the sauce. Season to taste with salt and pepper.

Serve calf's liver over Velvety Mashed Potatoes and spoon pan sauce over the top to just wet the liver. Top with crispy sage leaves and pancetta.

I KNOW, YOU HATE LIVER!
IF YOU CAN TELL ME THE
LAST TIME YOU ACTUALLY
HAD IT, I'LL LET YOU SLIDE.

SALMON WITH PICKLED
CUCUMBERS, DATES, AND HONEYED YOGURT

serves 2 • time: 45 minutes

I encourage you to do your part to stop harmful environmental and ecological practices by buying only wild salmon, preferably that which has been line-caught. Farmed salmon, in many cases, are pumped full of red dye to make them "salmon colored." That should be enough for you to realize that those farmed fish aren't the kind you want to put in your stomach. Buying smart will help the environment and make a big difference in the flavors you put on your plate.

Pickled Cucumbers and Dates

½ cup rice wine vinegar
¼ cup sugar
1 hothouse English cucumber, sliced
1 cup Medjool dates, split lengthwise and stones removed
1 red hot chile, finely sliced

Honeyed Yogurt

1 tablespoon honey
1 cup unsweetened Greek yogurt
1 teaspoon lemon juice
   Extra-virgin olive oil

2 8-ounce salmon fillets, skin on
   Kosher salt and freshly ground black pepper
   Extra-virgin olive oil
½ cup fresh mint leaves

For the Pickled Cucumbers and Dates, in a medium bowl combine the vinegar and sugar, stirring until dissolved. Add cucumber, dates, and chile and stir to coat evenly. Marinate in the refrigerator while preparing the yogurt and salmon.

For the Honeyed Yogurt, in a small bowl combine the honey, yogurt, and lemon juice, whisking to mix. Drizzle with oil. Place in the refrigerator until ready to serve.

Check salmon for bones and use tweezers to remove any you find. Season both sides of the fillets with salt and pepper. In a large sauté pan heat a 2-count of olive oil (about 2 tablespoons) over high heat. Add the fillets, skin sides down, and cook for 4 minutes without moving so the skin gets crispy. Turn the salmon and cook the flesh side for 30 seconds before removing and setting on a plate.

Serve salmon with Pickled Cucumbers and Dates and a smear of Honeyed Yogurt. Garnish with mint leaves.

SHRIMP SCAMPI WITH LINGUINE | serves 4 to 6 • time: 50 minutes

Creamy, garlicky, succulent shrimp are a match made in heaven for long, thin linguine. This Italian staple will forever find a place in your heart after you try my version.

1 pound dry linguine
4 tablespoons unsalted butter
2 tablespoons extra-virgin olive oil
2 shallots, finely diced
2 garlic cloves, minced
  Pinch red pepper flakes
1 pound large shrimp, peeled and deveined
  Kosher salt and freshly ground black pepper
½ cup dry white wine
1 28-ounce can whole San Marzano tomatoes
1 lemon, juice only
  Extra-virgin olive oil
¼ cup torn fresh basil leaves, for garnish

In a large stockpot of boiling salted water, add the linguine, stirring to make sure the pasta separates. When the water returns to a boil, cook for 6 to 8 minutes until the pasta is not quite done. Drain; set aside.

In a large sauté pan combine 2 tablespoons of the butter and the 2 tablespoons oil and place over medium-high heat to melt butter. Add shallots, garlic, and crushed red pepper; sauté for 3 to 4 minutes, until the shallots are translucent. Season the shrimp with salt and pepper; add to the skillet and cook for 2 to 3 minutes or until shrimp turn pink. Remove shrimp and keep warm. Add wine, tomatoes, and lemon juice to the skillet, crushing tomatoes with the back of a wooden spoon. Bring mixture to a boil. Reduce heat and simmer for 15 minutes to reduce the liquid. Return the shrimp to the skillet along with the cooked pasta. Stir well and season with salt and pepper. Drizzle lightly with olive oil and garnish with torn basil leaves.

SHRIMP WITH
SUGAR SNAP PEAS AND CASHEW BUTTER | serves 4 • time: 35 minutes

Asian flavors are at their freshest in this shrimp dish that offers a beautiful presentation. Cashew butter, ginger, garlic, sesame, sambal, and jasmine make for a depth of flavor that elevates this stir-fry above any you might have tried before. Sweet shrimp and peas make a nice starting point, and it explodes with flavor from there.

1   stick unsalted butter
½   cup roasted cashews
2   tablespoons toasted sesame oil
1   tablespoon minced ginger
1   tablespoon minced garlic
1   teaspoon sambal chile paste
1   pound medium shrimp, peeled and deveined with tails on
1   cup sugar snap peas, finely sliced
¾   cup soy sauce
½   lemon, juice only
2   tablespoons brown sugar
2   cups cooked jasmine rice, to serve
     Fresh cilantro, for garnish
     Scallions, cut into thin strips, for garnish

For cashew butter, in a food processor combine butter and roasted cashews and pulse until well combined. On a piece of parchment paper, form cashew butter into a log shape. Roll the parchment paper around the butter and twist the ends. Refrigerate until ready to use.

In a large sauté pan heat sesame oil, ginger, garlic, and sambal paste over high heat; toast until fragrant. Toss in shrimp and sauté until shrimp turn pink. Remove shrimp and set aside on a plate. Add sliced sugar snap peas to the pan, then add soy sauce, lemon juice, and brown sugar. Cook until peas are crisp-tender. Toss shrimp back in the pan to combine.

Serve over rice with a spoonful of cashew butter and garnish with fresh cilantro and cut scallions.

LOBSTER CAKES WITH
LEMON AÏOLI AND BACON FRISÉE SALAD | serves 2 to 4 • time: 50 minutes

These are called lobster cakes, not bread cakes, not batter cakes, not filler cakes. Load them up with plenty of fresh, sweet, luxurious lobster meat and sear them in a sauté pan. The lobster will bind but not cake, and you will be amazed at how light these feel, particularly with a bit of the fresh and bright aïoli. Lobster is the star here, and I like to treat it as such.

2   slices fresh white bread
1   pound fresh lobster meat, picked into large lumps
       (or 2 whole poached tails)
1   egg white
¼   cup store-bought mayonnaise
     Kosher salt and freshly ground black pepper
     Extra-virgin olive oil
4   slices bacon, cut into lardoons (narrow strips)
1   head frisée, torn
1   lemon, cut in half
1   recipe Lemon Aïoli (see recipe, below)

Remove crusts from bread; in a food processor process bread until it resembles coarse crumbs. In a large bowl combine bread crumbs, lobster, egg white, and mayonnaise; season with salt and pepper and stir to combine. The mixture should just hold together in a ball in the palm of your hand. Form into 4 large cakes. In a large sauté pan add a 3-count of oil (about 3 tablespoons). Heat oil over medium heat and fry cakes until they are golden brown, turning once.

In a large sauté pan cook bacon over medium heat for 8 to 10 minutes, until crispy. In a large salad bowl toss warm bacon together with frisée. Drizzle with oil and a squeeze of lemon juice, and season with salt and pepper. Serve lobster cakes with salad and Lemon Aïoli. Lightly drizzle additional olive oil on serving plates.

LEMON AÏOLI In a blender combine 1 tablespoon whole-grain mustard; ¼ cup sour cream; ¼ cup store-bought mayonnaise; ½ garlic clove, peeled and minced; ½ cup extra-virgin olive oil; 1 tablespoon lemon juice; 1 teaspoon kosher salt; and 5 turns of freshly ground black pepper. Process until smooth and creamy. Season with kosher salt and freshly ground pepper. Refrigerate until ready to serve.

POTATO GNOCCHI WITH BRAISED SWISS CHARD AND POMEGRANATE BROWN BUTTER

serves 6 to 8 • time: 2 hours 20 minutes

I learned this recipe while working at F. Illi Ponti in New York City back in the day and I have been making these gnocchi ever since. Try a new technique when making these dumplings by giving them some color and texture in the sauté pan after boiling. Light and fluffy on the inside with a savory crust on the outside. The brown butter benefits from the tartness of the pomegranate as it cuts through the rich and satisfying dumplings, while the earthy greens round it out for a really hearty vegetarian dish.

Gnocchi

- 2 pounds russet potatoes
- ½ cup grated Parmigiano-Reggiano
- 12 ounces fresh ricotta, drained
- ¼ teaspoon freshly grated nutmeg
- 2½ cups all-purpose flour
  Kosher salt and freshly ground black pepper
- 1 stick unsalted butter

Pomegranate Brown Butter Sauce

- 2 sticks unsalted butter
- 4 cups pomegranate juice, reduced
  Kosher salt and freshly ground black pepper

Braised Swiss Chard
Extra-virgin olive oil
4 garlic cloves, peeled and minced
2 small onions, diced
2 bunches Swiss chard, roughly chopped
2 quarts vegetable broth
Kosher salt and freshly ground black pepper
¼ cup apple cider vinegar
2 tablespoons unsalted butter

¼ cup fresh pomegranate seeds, for garnish (optional)
¼ cup Parmigiano-Reggiano shavings, for garnish

For the Gnocchi, preheat oven to 350°F. Arrange potatoes on a roasting tray and prick all over with a fork to make holes. Roast potatoes for 45 to 50 minutes, until the flesh is tender enough to scoop out with a spoon. When cool enough to handle, scoop the warm flesh into a food processor and puree with the grated Parmigiano-Reggiano. Refrigerate until completely cool.

In a large bowl fold together the potato puree, drained ricotta, and nutmeg. Fold in the flour, 1 cup at a time. Season with salt and pepper and mix until a soft dough forms. (Do not overwork dough or it will be tough.) Flour a surface and roll dough into a rope 1 inch in diameter. Cut into small pillow shapes.

Bring a large pot of salted water to a boil. Add gnocchi and cook until they float. Drain well and transfer gnocchi to a sheet tray. Refrigerate until cool. When gnocchi are cool, melt the 1 stick butter in a large nonstick sauté pan over high heat. Add gnocchi and sauté until brown. Set aside.

For the Pomegranate Brown Butter Sauce, brown the 2 sticks butter in a large saucepan over medium-low heat until it turns a hazelnut color (the butter solids should be brown and aromatic). Meanwhile, in a large saucepan reduce pomegranate juice over medium-high heat until syrupy. Add pomegranate reduction to brown butter. Swirl pan to combine ingredients; season lightly with salt and pepper.

For the Braised Swiss Chard, in a small stockpot heat a 2-count of olive oil (about 2 tablespoons) over medium heat. Add garlic and onions; sauté for 2 to 3 minutes or until fragrant. Add Swiss chard and toss a few times. Add vegetable broth. Season with salt and pepper; simmer for 5 to 6 minutes, until Swiss chard is wilted and tender. Stir in vinegar and the 2 tablespoons butter. Toss well to combine.

Serve Braised Swiss Chard with Gnocchi and top with Pomegranate Brown Butter Sauce. If you like, garnish with pomegranate seeds and sprinkle with Parmigiano-Reggiano shavings.

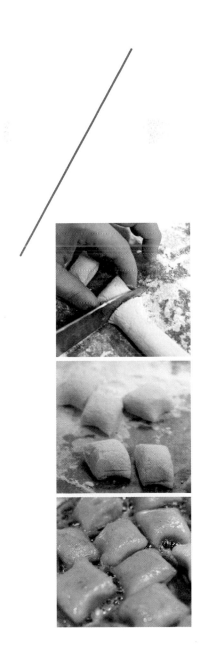

GRILLED CHEESE
(SMOKED MOZZARELLA AND BASIL PESTO) | serves 2 • time: 30 minutes

Sautéed cheese sandwich doesn't sound right, so I'm sticking with tradition of calling it "grilled cheese." But the perfect grilled cheese is a true test of one's sauté skills as you have to get that golden brown crust just right while getting the creamy, smoky cheese to melt on the inside before the bread starts to burn. This fresh basil pesto is absolutely delicious and is the key to taking the familiar sandwich to a new level.

Basil Pesto

2 cups fresh basil leaves
1 cup fresh Italian flat-leaf parsley leaves
½ cup grated Parmigiano-Reggiano
½ cup pine nuts, toasted
3 garlic cloves, peeled and roughly chopped
¼ teaspoon kosher salt
½ cup extra-virgin olive oil

Grilled Cheese Sandwiches

4 slices white sandwich bread
4 thick-cut slices smoked mozzarella
   Freshly ground black pepper
2 tablespoons unsalted butter
1 garlic clove, peeled

For the Basil Pesto, in a food processor combine basil, parsley, Parmigiano-Reggiano, pine nuts, garlic, salt, and oil and pulse until well combined but still rough in texture.

Assemble sandwiches by smearing one side of each bread slice with pesto. Layer the mozzarella slices over the pesto on half of the bread slices. Season with a few turns of freshly ground black pepper. Place the remaining bread slices, pesto sides down, over cheese to make the sandwiches.

In large sauté pan melt butter over medium heat. Add sandwiches and cook 2 to 3 minutes per side, until golden brown and crispy. Remove from pan and rub toasted bread with the garlic clove.

BRAISE

NOW LET'S TALK ABOUT BRAISING, A COOKING TECHNIQUE WITH WHICH YOU MIGHT NOT BE SO FAMILIAR. (OR SO YOU THINK.)

Remember Granny's pot roast, the one you loved so much as a kid? She braised that big hunk of beef until it became that tender, flavorful comfort classic that always brings you right back home.

Braising is a simple concept that can create an amazing combination of flavors and soft, luxurious textures. In a braise, we are going to do a simple simmer, cooking our food in a small amount of liquid. When you bring up the heated liquid to a certain temperature, what you are really creating is a flavor whirlpool with all of the tastiness from the liquid interacting with the flavors of the food in a continuous cycle. And this is important to remember, because how you season and flavor your liquid will be a big part of your dish. Play around with aromatics, different liquids, and herbs, and you will create exciting combinations.

Now here's where it really gets interesting and we get into what sets braising apart from other cooking methods: Some of the most spectacular braising results come when you tackle an otherwise unruly piece of meat. You know what pieces I mean—the big hunk of beef at the grocery store that kind of looks like an oversize New York Strip steak but is about $2.99 per pound instead of $12.99. Braise it. Long cooking times and high temperatures used in braising bigger, tougher cuts of meat are absolutely perfect for breaking down all of the proteins and fats so that they melt into the meat and the liquid. So save yourself a couple of bucks and create something amazing in the meantime.

COUNTRY SPARE RIBS AND
MUSTARD GREENS BRAISED IN APPLE CIDER | serves 6 to 8 • time: 3 hours

Country ribs aren't really ribs at all. In fact, they are closer to pork chops than anything else. Nonetheless, they take well to a braise and in this case, they really absorb the sweetness of the apple cider. The actual rib meat is lean but it is situated between layers of fat. A long, slow braising serves to break it all down. The result is a flavor exchange and the enriching and thickening of the sweet apple cider braising liquid.

1 4-pound pork rib roast
   Extra-virgin olive oil
   Kosher salt and freshly ground black pepper
2 bunches mustard greens
1 bunch fresh thyme sprigs (about 16 sprigs)
1 bulb garlic, cut through the equator (horizontally)
½ gallon apple juice
½ cup apple cider vinegar
1 recipe Velvety Mashed Potatoes (see recipe, below)

Preheat oven to 350°F. Drizzle oil all over rib roast and season with salt and pepper. Lay rib roast, bone side down, in a large roasting pan. Spread mustard greens around the pan, then scatter the thyme and place the garlic bulb halves in the pan. Pour in apple juice and cider vinegar. Cover with aluminum foil and braise for 2½ hours, basting every 30 minutes.

Remove the foil and baste the meat. Cook, uncovered, for 30 minutes more until the meat's surface caramelizes and the liquid reduces and forms a sticky glaze on the meat. Set ribs aside. Remove and discard thyme. Squeeze the garlic pulp into a blender along with the juices from the pan, and puree. Serve ribs over mustard greens with braising liquid and Velvety Mashed Potatoes.

VELVETY MASHED POTATOES In a small saucepan warm 1 cup heavy whipping cream and 4 tablespoons unsalted butter over medium heat until the butter melts; set aside. Peel 4 large Yukon gold potatoes; put in a medium saucepan and cover with cold water. Bring to a boil, then reduce the heat. Add 1 teaspoon kosher salt and simmer for 15 to 20 minutes, until the potatoes are very tender. Drain well. Pass the potatoes through a food mill or a ricer back into the saucepan. Stir in the warm cream and butter mixture until the cream is absorbed and the mixture is smooth. Stir in ¼ cup extra-virgin olive oil. Season with kosher salt and pepper.

POT ROAST RISOTTO

serves 6 • time: 3 hours 45 minutes

Risotto is much more than just a rice dish—in fact, this one is a complete meal! The rice contains a lot of natural starch that is released when cooked the right way, creating a creaminess that you don't get if you just boil it. When you braise beef shoulder, the same effect takes place as the fats break down and melt into the liquid. Rich, creamy, and hearty, this dish is truly satisfying.

Pot Roast

3   pounds beef shoulder
    Extra-virgin olive oil
    Kosher salt and freshly ground black pepper
3   garlic cloves, peeled and smashed
4   sprigs fresh thyme
2   bay leaves
2   large onions, sliced
1   cup dry red wine
2   quarts beef broth

Risotto

3   tablespoons extra-virgin olive oil
1   medium onion, finely chopped
2   cups Arborio rice
1   cup dry white wine
4   sprigs fresh thyme, leaves only
    Kosher salt and freshly ground black pepper
2   tablespoons unsalted butter
½   cup freshly grated Parmigiano-Reggiano
½   cup chopped fresh Italian flat-leaf parsley

Preheat oven to 350°F. For the Pot Roast, drizzle the meat with oil and season all over with salt and pepper. In a large heavy pot or Dutch oven heat a 3-count of oil (about 3 tablespoons) over medium-high heat. Add the beef and sear all over until brown and a crust forms. Add the garlic, thyme, bay leaves, and onion to the pot. Pour in the red wine and beef broth. Cover the pot and transfer to the preheated oven. Braise about 3 hours, basting every 30 minutes with the pan juices, until the beef is fork-tender. Transfer the meat and onions to a clean bowl; set aside and keep warm. Strain the braising liquid and skim the fat. (If you like, set aside bay leaves for garnish.) Reserve 8 cups braising liquid (keep liquid hot; it will be used for the risotto).

For the Risotto, in a large deep skillet heat the 3 tablespoons olive oil over medium heat. Add onion and cook for 5 minutes until soft. Stir in the rice, coating all the grains with the oil. Add white wine and thyme and cook until most of the wine has evaporated. Ladle in 1 cup of the

hot reserved braising liquid. Using a wooden spoon, stir constantly until most of the liquid has been absorbed. Keep adding liquid, 1 cup at a time, and stirring until absorbed. After 10 to 15 minutes, test the rice. It should be cooked and creamy but still have a slight bite to it. (You may not need all of the liquid.) When risotto is done, season with salt and pepper; stir in butter and most of the Parmigiano-Reggiano, reserving a little for the garnish. Remove from heat and cover. Just before serving, fold in chopped parsley. Serve sliced Pot Roast with Risotto. Shower with more fresh parsley and grated Parmigiano-Reggiano. If you like, garnish with reserved bay leaves.

VEAL BRAISED IN MILK AND
HONEY WITH BUTTERED TURNIPS

serves 6 to 8 • time: 3 hours 30 minutes

This dish is one of those that comes out above and beyond all your expectations. The milk and honey braising liquid is sweet and really enhances the richness of the lean veal. The veal stays tender and the resulting braising liquid creates a beautiful, sweet gravy of sorts that you will want to eat with a spoon.

Extra-virgin olive oil
4 pounds veal shoulder, tied
Kosher salt and freshly ground black pepper
4 garlic cloves, peeled
¼ bunch fresh thyme sprigs (about 4 sprigs)
4 to 5 dried porcini mushrooms
½ gallon milk
3 tablespoons honey
1 recipe Buttered Turnips (see recipe, below)

Preheat oven to 350°F. In a large heavy pot or Dutch oven heat a 3-count of olive oil (about 3 tablespoons) over medium-high heat. Season veal with plenty of salt and pepper. Add veal to pot, cook and turn until brown all over and a crust forms. Add garlic, thyme, and mushrooms. Pour in the milk and stir in the honey. Cover and braise about 3 hours, until the veal is fork-tender.

Remove veal from pot and set aside. Carefully pour small batches of the braising liquid, along with garlic and mushrooms, into a blender. Tightly hold the lid in place with a kitchen towel and puree until slightly thickened and silky smooth. Continue with the rest of the braising liquid, mushrooms, and garlic. Season to taste with pepper and pour over meat. Serve with Buttered Turnips.

BUTTERED TURNIPS Preheat oven to 350°F. Peel and quarter 6 medium-size turnips. Place turnips on a roasting tray; drizzle with extra-virgin olive oil and season with kosher salt. Roast for 25 to 30 minutes until just tender. Toss roasted turnips in a large bowl with 2 tablespoons unsalted butter and 2 tablespoons chopped fresh Italian flat-leaf parsley so they are evenly coated and glossy. Season with kosher salt.

SLOW-BRAISED MEATBALLS
WITH CRANBERRY SAUCE AND EGG NOODLES | serves 6 to 8 • time: 1 hour

These aren't your typical goodfella's meatballs. You can look to Sweden for the inspiration here with the sweet cranberry sauce serving as a substitute for the traditional lingonberries.

Meatballs
Extra-virgin olive oil
1   medium onion, chopped
4   garlic cloves, peeled and minced
4   sprigs fresh thyme, leaves only
2   slices white sandwich bread
1   cup whole milk
1   pound ground beef
1   pound ground veal
1   pound ground pork
1   large egg
    Kosher salt and freshly ground black pepper
1   750-milliliter bottle red wine
1   quart reduced-sodium beef broth
1   tablespoon honey
1   tablespoon Dijon mustard
½   teaspoon caraway seeds
2   tablespoons crème fraîche

Cranberry Sauce
10   ounces frozen cranberries
1   orange, juice only

Noodles
1   pound dried egg noodles
2   tablespoons extra-virgin olive oil
¼   cup chopped fresh dill

Preheat oven to 325°F. For Meatballs, in a medium sauté pan heat a 2-count of olive oil (about 2 tablespoons) over medium heat. Add onions, garlic, and thyme. Cook for 10 to 12 minutes until onions are caramelized. Remove crusts from bread and soak bread in milk. In a large bowl combine beef, veal, and pork. Add soaked bread, egg, and cooked onion, garlic, and thyme. Season with salt and pepper and mix well to combine.

In a heavy roasting dish heat a 3-count of olive oil (about 3 tablespoons) over medium-high heat. Add meatballs and cook for 3 to 5 minutes, browning all over. Turn the heat to high and add wine and broth. Bring to a boil; remove from heat. Cover dish with

WHAT YOU ARE REALLY CREATING IS A FLAVOR WHIRLPOOL WITH ALL OF THE TASTINESS FROM THE LIQUID INTERACTING WITH THE FLAVORS OF THE FOOD IN A CONTINUOUS CYCLE.

aluminum foil and braise for 45 minutes, basting the meatballs every 20 minutes. If all the liquid evaporates, add more broth as you go. When done, remove the meatballs and set aside. Set the pan with the braising liquid on the stovetop over medium heat and add honey, mustard, and caraway seeds. Simmer to reduce mixture until it is thick and syrupy. Stir in crème fraîche and season with salt and pepper.

For the Cranberry Sauce, in a small saucepan combine cranberries with orange juice. Simmer about 10 minutes, until sauce is pulpy and thick. Remove from heat.

Meanwhile, in a large pot of salted boiling water, cook noodles according to package directions. Drain; toss with oil and dill. To serve, top noodles with meatballs and sauce. Serve the Cranberry Sauce on the side.

LAMB SHANK STEW
WITH RUSSET POTATO TOP

serves 6 to 8 • time: 3 hours 25 minutes

When braising lamb shanks, all of the collagen in the bones contributes to the braising liquid, and that means richness and deep flavor. Lamb stew takes advantage of this delicious gelatin, which changes the composition of the entire dish. Give this recipe a shot on a cold, snowy night.

Stew

- ¼ cup all-purpose flour
  Kosher salt and freshly ground black pepper
- 6 lamb shanks (about 8 ounces each), cut in half
  Extra-virgin olive oil
- 2 garlic cloves, peeled and smashed
- 2 large carrots, cut into chunks
- 1 large onion, cut into chunks
- 2 whole cloves
- ¼ bunch fresh thyme sprigs
- 1 bay leaf
- 1 750-milliliter bottle red wine
- 1 quart reduced-sodium beef broth
- 1 cup barley

Garlic-Parsley Butter

- 1 stick unsalted butter, room temperature
- ¼ bunch fresh Italian flat-leaf parsley, leaves only, chopped
- 2 garlic cloves, peeled and minced
  Kosher salt and freshly ground black pepper

6 large russet potatoes

Preheat oven to 350°F. For the Stew, season flour with salt and pepper, then lightly dredge the shank pieces in flour. In a large heavy pot or Dutch oven heat a 2-count of olive oil (about 2 tablespoons) over medium-high heat. Carefully add the shanks to the pot and brown all over. Add garlic, carrots, onion, cloves, thyme, and bay leaf. Cook for 2 to 3 minutes, browning the vegetables, then add wine, broth, and barley. Cover and braise in the preheated oven for 2 hours.

For the Garlic-Parsley Butter, in a bowl combine butter with parsley and garlic; season with salt and pepper and stir to mix. Set aside.

Peel the potatoes and cut in half lengthwise. After the stew has been braising for 2 hours, remove from oven and arrange potatoes on top to completely cover the stew (you may have to cut some of the potato pieces smaller to fit). Place back in the oven and bake, uncovered, for 30 minutes more. Baste with Garlic-Parsley Butter; return to the oven and bake for 30 minutes more, until the top crust is golden and bubbly.

SOME OF THE MOST SPECTACULAR BRAISING RESULTS COME WHEN YOU TACKLE AN OTHERWISE UNRULY PIECE OF MEAT.

COQ AU VIN | serves 4 • time: 1 hour 45 minutes

My local market was fresh out of roosters the day I planned to make this traditional French dish, but a chicken did just fine. Back in the day, the French cooked older roosters to take advantage of the extra connective tissue they had, which in turn contributed to the consistency of the broth. But that's not practical or necessary today, and we can achieve a rich, satisfying broth and deeply flavored chicken with just the right amount of herbs, seasonings, and of course, wine. This is a classic braise that's worth perfecting.

1   3- to 4-pound whole free-range chicken
     Extra-virgin olive oil
¼   cup all-purpose flour
     Kosher salt and freshly ground black pepper
2   carrots, cut into chunks
1   large onion, cut into chunks
3   ribs celery, cut into chunks
¼   bunch fresh thyme sprigs (about 4 sprigs)
1   bay leaf
1   750-milliliter bottle dry red wine
4   thick-cut slices bacon, cut into lardoons (long, thin strips)
1   cup pearl onions, peeled
1   cup button mushrooms, halved
3   tablespoons chopped fresh Italian flat-leaf parsley

Cut chicken into 10 pieces: 2 legs, 2 thighs, 2 wings, and a quartered breast. In a large heavy pot or Dutch oven heat a 3-count of olive oil (about 3 tablespoons) over medium heat. Season flour with salt and pepper. Dredge chicken pieces in flour mixture a few pieces at a time. Cook for 7 to 10 minutes, browning all over. Add carrots, onion, celery, thyme, and bay leaf. Pour in wine and deglaze the pan, using a wooden spoon to scrape up any brown bits from the bottom of the pan. Cover and simmer over low heat for 1 hour. Remove lid and transfer chicken to a clean platter. Strain the braising liquid and discard the vegetables. Simmer the liquid about 15 minutes until reduced, syrupy, and slightly glossy. Place chicken back in the liquid.

In a large sauté pan cook bacon over medium heat to render the fat. Once bacon is crispy, remove from pan and drain on paper towels, reserving the fat in the pan. Add pearl onions to the pan and sauté until golden and caramelized; season with salt and pepper and set aside. Cook the mushrooms in the same pan; season well with salt and pepper. Toss bacon, onions, and mushrooms back into the pot with the chicken. Sprinkle with chopped parsley and serve.

DUCK AND PUMPKIN GREEN CURRY

serves 4 • time: 2 hours 15 minutes

I am in love with this curry dish, and I know you will be too. Green curry is a traditional Thai curry with a sweet coconut milk base. The soft squash soaks up the delicious spices, and the duck's fat melts right into the dish. I use duck here because it is rich and flavorful enough to stand up to the strength of the curry, but you can substitute chicken as well. Take a look at the gorgeous color!

- 1   4- to 5-pound whole duck
      Extra-virgin olive oil
      Kosher salt and freshly ground black pepper
- 2   15-ounce cans coconut milk
- 2   star anise
- 3   cinnamon sticks
- 1   1-inch piece ginger
- 1   small pumpkin or large acorn squash, seeds removed, peeled, and cut into slices
- 2   tablespoons Thai green curry paste
- 2   bunches fresh cilantro
- 2   limes, juice only

- 2   cups steamed jasmine rice
      Lime wedges, to serve
      Fresh mint, to serve

Cut the duck into 8 pieces: 2 leg/thigh portions, 2 wings, and a quartered breast with bone attached. In a large heavy pot or Dutch oven heat a 2-count of olive oil (about 2 tablespoons) over medium heat. Season duck pieces with salt and pepper. Carefully add them to the pan and cook for 8 to 10 minutes, until golden brown all over. Add coconut milk, star anise, cinnamon, and ginger to the pot; cover and simmer for 1 hour. Add the squash and stir. Cover and cook for 30 minutes more, until the duck is tender and the squash is cooked. Remove 1 cup of the braising liquid.

In a blender combine the 1 cup braising liquid, the green curry paste, cilantro, and lime juice. Puree until a bright green mixture forms. Fold paste back into the pot of curry and season with salt and pepper to taste. Serve with steamed rice, lime wedges, and fresh mint.

BRAISING ISN'T ALWAYS ABOUT BIG CUTS OF MEAT OR THICK POULTRY PARTS. YOU CAN BRAISE EVEN THE MOST DELICATE OF PROTEINS.

SEA BASS WITH CLAMS IN LEMONY ESCAROLE | serves 4 • time: 45 minutes

Braising isn't always about big cuts of meat or thick poultry parts. You can braise even the most delicate of proteins, such as sea bass and clams, in a slow simmer just enough to cook them through and impart a bit of flavor. You'll pick up the nuances of your braising liquid here and the aromatics will really come into play. Try the lighter side of braising and note that the same principles apply.

- 1   quart reduced-sodium chicken broth
- ½   lemon, thinly sliced
- 1   garlic clove, peeled
- ¼   bunch fresh thyme sprigs (about 4 sprigs)
- 1   bay leaf
- 1   bunch escarole
- 16   small clams, washed and scrubbed
  Kosher salt and freshly ground black pepper
  Extra-virgin olive oil
- 4   slices (about 4 ounces) thinly sliced pancetta, cut into strips
- 1   pound filleted sea bass, cut into 4 pieces
- 2   tablespoons unsalted butter

Set a large heavy pot or Dutch oven over medium heat and add the chicken broth, lemon, garlic, thyme, and bay leaf. Bring to a boil, then add escarole and clams. Cover and simmer for 15 minutes, until clams open. Season with salt and pepper.

In a large nonstick sauté pan heat a 2-count of olive oil (about 2 tablespoons) over medium-high heat. Add pancetta and stir with a wooden spoon. Cook for 4 to 5 minutes, until pancetta is crispy and curls up; set aside on paper towels. Reserve pancetta fat in the pan.

Season sea bass with salt and pepper. Return pan to medium heat. Once oil is smoking, add fillets and don't move them for 3 minutes. Add butter to the pan, turn the fillets, and cook for 30 seconds before removing.

Divide escarole, clams, and broth among shallow bowls. Top with sea bass fillet and sprinkle crispy pancetta over the top.

FRY

IN THE SOUTH, WHERE I COME FROM, FRYING IS A WAY OF LIFE. I KNOW GUYS WHO COULD FRY A TIRE AND MAKE IT TASTE GOOD.

I'm a fan and I think frying gets a bad rap. You are not going to die a long, slow, painful death because you enjoyed some fried foods on Saturday night. In fact, if you know what you're doing, frying can add very little fat while sealing in flavor and moisture to reach new heights of enjoyment. In today's frying, we have replaced old-school animal fats with healthier vegetable oils such as olive, canola, safflower, and peanut. When the food hits the hot oil, it begins to form a crust (AGAIN, COLOR EQUALS FLAVOR) that essentially locks the moisture into the food. Because oil and water have different densities, the moisture stays in and the oil stays out.

Temperature is very important when frying, in that it dictates how your food is cooked and how much oil gets absorbed. Get out the thermometer and get ready to use it. Basically, bigger foods (like a turkey wing) are fried at lower temperatures for longer periods of time to allow for the food to cook through before the crust burns. Smaller, more delicate foods (such as sliced sweet potatoes) are fried hot and fast to get the crispness needed on the outside without absorbing oil. Another way food gets bogged down in oil is when you start coating it with heavy breading or batter before frying. I will give you a few ideas on how to create some savory, crispy crusts without ending up with a sponge. So let's get this hot, crispy, and delicious ball rolling …

FRIED CHICKEN WITH
BUTTERMILK CHERRY TOMATOES

serves 4 • time: 3 hours *(includes marinating)*

Fried chicken is as near and dear to my heart as anything. At the end of the day, I'm a Southern boy, and this fried chicken brings me right back to my childhood every time I even think about it. Perfect your frying technique on this one, and you'll be making it for years to come.

1   3- to 4-pound whole free-range chicken
2   cups buttermilk
2   tablespoons bottled hot sauce
3   cups all-purpose flour
2   tablespoons garlic powder
2   tablespoons onion powder
2   tablespoons sweet paprika
2   teaspoons cayenne pepper
    Kosher salt and freshly ground black pepper
    Peanut oil, for deep-frying
1   bunch ancho cress or other peppery lettuce
1   recipe Cherry Tomatoes with Buttermilk Blue Cheese
       (see recipe, below)

Cut the chicken into 10 pieces: 2 legs, 2 thighs, 2 wings, and a quartered breast. In a large bowl, combine buttermilk and hot sauce. Add chicken to buttermilk mixture. Cover with plastic wrap; set in the refrigerator for at least 2 hours or overnight.

On a large shallow plate combine the flour, garlic powder, onion powder, paprika, and cayenne pepper until well blended; season mixture with salt and black pepper. Drain the chicken pieces and dredge them in the flour mixture, coating both sides completely. Set chicken aside while you heat the oil.

Pour about 4 inches oil into a large heavy pot and heat to 375°F. Working in batches, add the chicken pieces (about 3 pieces at a time). Fry about 20 minutes, until golden brown and cooked through (170°F), turning the pieces once. Remove chicken from oil; drain on a kitchen towel or paper towels. Season with salt. Serve with ancho cress and Cherry Tomatoes with Buttermilk Blue Cheese dressing.

CHERRY TOMATOES WITH BUTTERMILK BLUE CHEESE In a medium bowl combine ½ cup crumbled blue cheese, ½ cup buttermilk, and 2 tablespoons extra-virgin olive oil, mashing with a fork to break up the cheese. Add 2 tablespoons fresh lemon juice and 1 bunch chives (about 16 chives), chopped. Season with salt and freshly ground black pepper. Slice 2 cups cherry tomatoes in half lengthwise and toss in the dressing.

FISH AND CHIPS WITH HOMEMADE TARTAR | serves 4 • time: 1 hour 20 minutes

Whenever I'm in London, the very first thing I do is head out for some fish and chips and a pint. The thing about fish and chips is that the batter has to be perfect; the fries just right. And over the years, I have developed what I believe to be the perfect combination. Skip the traditional vinegar and try this homemade tartar sauce.

4 large russet potatoes, scrubbed and rinsed
Vegetable oil, for deep-frying
Kosher salt and freshly ground black pepper
2 cups all-purpose flour, plus about 1 cup for dredging
½ cup cornstarch
2 tablespoons baking powder
1½ teaspoons kosher salt
2 egg yolks
1½ cups club soda
1 pound halibut fillets, cut into strips or pieces
Fresh Italian flat-leaf parsley leaves, for garnish
2 lemons, halved, for serving
1 recipe Homemade Tartar Sauce (see recipe, page 131)

Preheat oven to 350°F. Prick potatoes all over with a fork. Place the potatoes on a baking tray and bake for 30 to 45 minutes, until knife-tender. (If you like, this can be done the night before and potatoes can be refrigerated until ready to fry.) Cut each potato into 6 or 8 wedges, depending on the size. Pour about 4 inches oil into a large heavy pot and heat to 375°F. Fry half of the potato wedges at a time for 4 to 5 minutes, until crispy and brown. Drain on paper towels and season with salt. Set aside and keep warm.

In a large bowl combine the 2 cups flour, cornstarch, baking powder, and 1½ teaspoons salt. Make a well in the center and add egg yolks. Gradually whisk in club soda, working your way out from the center to form a smooth batter.

Season about 1 cup flour with salt and pepper. Dredge the fish fillets in seasoned flour, coating both sides, then dip in batter. Fry a few pieces at a time in 375°F oil for 4 to 5 minutes, until crispy and golden brown. Drain on paper towels and season with salt.

When fish is done, place parsley leaves in hot oil. Fry leaves for 15 seconds, until just crispy and slightly translucent. Remove from oil with a slotted spoon; drain on paper towels. Serve fish with lemon halves, crispy fried parsley leaves, and Homemade Tartar Sauce.

HOMEMADE TARTAR SAUCE In a small bowl combine ½ cup store-bought mayonnaise; ½ cup sour cream; 2 tablespoons capers, chopped; ¼ cup chopped cornichons; 2 tablespoons chopped fresh Italian flat-leaf parsley; 1 tablespoon finely chopped fresh tarragon; and ½ lemon, juice only. Set aside in the refrigerator for 10 to 15 minutes before serving to let the flavors come together.

CRISPY COCONUT SHRIMP LETTUCE WRAPS WITH SPICY PEANUT DIPPING SAUCE | serves 4 to 6 • time: 45 minutes

Here's another Asian-inspired dish that brings together Thai and tropical flavors. Fried coconut shrimp is often done but seldom done right. We have all been to that chain restaurant that overbatters, overfries, and then sweetens their shriveled shrimp to oblivion—you may even have enjoyed it! But in this recipe we are working with the natural sweetness of the coconut to balance perfectly with the spicy dipping sauce. The result will be the best coconut shrimp you've ever had.

Spicy Peanut Dipping Sauce

- ¼ cup toasted sesame oil
- 1 teaspoon grated fresh ginger
- 1 garlic clove, peeled and minced
- ½ cup peanut butter
- 2 tablespoons Sriracha hot sauce
- 2 tablespoons brown sugar
  Reduced-sodium soy sauce
- ¼ cup rice wine vinegar
- ⅓ cup hot water

Coconut Shrimp

- 12 large shrimp, peeled, deveined, and butterflied
- 1 cup all-purpose flour
  Kosher salt and freshly ground black pepper
- 2 eggs, beaten
- 2 cups unsweetened shredded coconut
  Vegetable oil, for deep-frying

- 1 head Bibb lettuce, separated
- 1 English cucumber, cut into sticks
- 2 limes, cut into wedges
- 1 bunch snow pea shoots

For the Spicy Peanut Dipping Sauce, pour sesame oil in a small saucepan and heat over low heat. Add the ginger and garlic; cook for 2 minutes, until fragrant. Combine the remaining sauce ingredients in a blender; blend to combine. Add the warmed sesame oil mixture to blender. Blend until light and creamy, adding more hot water, if necessary, to achieve a smooth dipping consistency.

Lay the butterflied shrimp flat on a cutting board. Place the flat side of a chef's knife on the shrimp; gently pound to flatten. Thread one butterflied shrimp onto each bamboo skewer, so shrimp lays flat. Set aside.

Place flour on a large shallow plate; season with salt and pepper. Place beaten eggs in a shallow bowl. Place coconut on a large shallow plate; season with salt and pepper. Coat the shrimp in flour, shaking off the excess. Dip shrimp in egg, then coconut, coating both sides. Place on a baking tray and set aside in the refrigerator for 15 minutes to allow the coating to set before frying.

Pour about 4 inches oil into a large heavy pot and heat to 375°F. Place the shrimp end of each skewer in hot oil and fry for 2 to 3 minutes, until golden and crispy. Remove with tongs.

To serve, arrange Bibb lettuce leaves, cucumber sticks, lime wedges, and snow pea shoots on a large plate. Serve with coconut shrimp and dipping sauce so wraps can be assembled as desired.

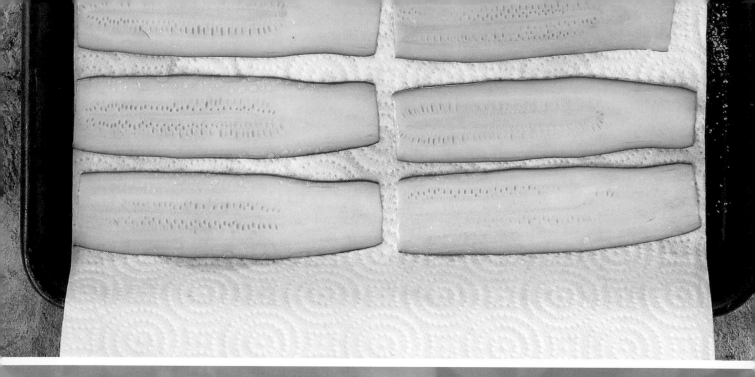

IN THE SOUTH, WHERE I COME FROM, FRYING IS A WAY OF LIFE. I KNOW GUYS WHO COULD FRY A TIRE AND MAKE IT TASTE GOOD.

ZUCCHINI CRAB
FRITTERS WITH GRAPEFRUIT AÏOLI | serves 4 to 6 • time: 50 minutes

The word "fritter" applies to just about anything fried in batter, as it is a combination of the words "fried" and "batter." Roadside stands around the world dish up fritters with any number of ingredients. Batter-fry a slice of sweet potato and call it a fritter. Simple enough, right? But dress it up with beautiful fresh California Dungeness crab and delicate zucchini, and you've taken the fritter far beyond its roadside roots.

2   zucchini
    Kosher salt and freshly ground black pepper
1   pound fresh lump crabmeat
1   egg white
1   cup all-purpose flour
2   cups panko (Japanese bread crumbs)
2   eggs, beaten
    Vegetable oil, for deep-frying

    Grapefruit Aïoli
1   grapefruit, juice and 1 teaspoon zest
½   cup store bought mayonnaise
½   cup sour cream

Using a mandoline, slice the zucchini lengthwise into long, thin strips. Lay the strips in a single layer on a tray lined with a kitchen towel or a paper towel. Sprinkle salt over the zucchini strips and set aside. (Adding salt draws out the moisture and makes the strips pliable.)

Drain the crab of any excess moisture, then combine with egg white in a bowl. Season with salt and pepper. Place a spoonful of crab mixture on one end of each zucchini slice. Roll up, starting with end that has crab mixture. Place rolls, seam sides down, on a flat surface. Place flour on a large shallow plate; season with salt and pepper. Place panko on large shallow plate; season with salt and pepper. Place beaten eggs in a shallow bowl. Coat the fritters in seasoned flour, shaking off the excess. Dip fritters in egg, and then in seasoned panko, coating completely. Place on a baking tray and set aside in the refrigerator for 15 minutes to let the coating set.

Pour 2 to 3 inches oil into a large heavy pot and heat to 350°F. Fry a few rolls at a time for about 4 minutes, until crumbs are golden. Remove rolls from oil; drain on paper towels.

For the Grapefruit Aïoli, in a small saucepan simmer grapefruit juice and zest until reduced by half. Remove from heat and cool. Combine mayonnaise, sour cream, and cooled grapefruit reduction in a blender. Blend until combined. Serve with warm fritters.

CORN CHOWDER WITH
CHORIZO AND HOG ISLAND FRIED OYSTERS

serves 4 • time: 1 hour 15 minutes

Sometimes the beauty in a fried dish is an exercise in restraint. As a component of another dish, such as this silky corn chowder, the crispy fried oyster really pops as a point of contrast. The best oysters in the country are coming out of the Hog Island Oyster Company, just up the coast from my house, and the briny taste of the sea really shines against the creaminess of the chowder.

Corn Chowder

- 4 cups milk
- 1 cup heavy whipping cream
- 4 ears sweet corn, husked
- 2 garlic cloves, peeled
- 4 sprigs fresh thyme
  Kosher salt and freshly ground black pepper
- 2 links Spanish chorizo (about ½ pound), casings removed, and chopped in to small cubes
  Extra-virgin olive oil

Fried Oysters

- 4 large oysters (use a locally farmed variety), shucked
- ¾ cup fine ground cornmeal
- ¼ cup cornstarch
- 2 tablespoons baking powder
- 1 teaspoon kosher salt
- 1 egg yolk
- ¾ cup club soda, chilled

  Vegetable oil, for deep-frying
  Kosher salt
  Fresh Italian flat-leaf parsley, for garnish

For the Corn Chowder, in a large pot heat milk and cream over low heat. Add corn, garlic, and thyme. Bring to a boil; simmer for 5 minutes. Cover and shut off heat to allow the milk to steep with the corn. Once steeped (about 15 minutes), cut the corn off the cobs. Strain the milk mixture with a fine sieve and transfer to a blender. Add the corn to the strained milk and puree. Season to taste with salt and pepper. Keep warm.

In a skillet cook chorizo and a 2-count of olive oil (about 2 tablespoons) over low heat for 2 to 3 minutes to render fat and infuse the oil.

For the oysters, in a bowl combine cornmeal, cornstarch, baking powder, and salt. Make a well in the center and add yolk. Gradually whisk in club soda, slowly working your way out from the center to form a smooth batter.

Pour about 2 inches oil into a large heavy pot and heat to 375°F. Dip oysters in the batter and fry for 1½ to 2 minutes, until golden and puffy. Drain on paper towels and season with salt.

Serve Corn Chowder topped with chorizo, a splash of infused chorizo oil, a fried oyster, and parsley.

MONTEREY BAY CALAMARI WITH CHILE-LIME SALT serves 4 • time: 30 minutes

California's first city, Monterey, is a world-class tourist destination that has its roots in fishing. Sardines, salmon, abalone—you name it, it's part of Monterey's history. But in my opinion, the local calamari is what really stands out. In this recipe, the tart salt with a hint of heat really highlights the sweet, tender squid but doesn't overpower it. Fresh, tender calamari really is quite a treat.

Vegetable oil for deep-frying
½ cup all-purpose flour
Kosher salt and freshly ground black pepper
1 pound cleaned Monterey calamari, bodies and tentacles
1 recipe Chile-Lime Salt (see recipe, below)
Limes, halved, for serving

Pour 3 to 4 inches oil into a large heavy pot and heat to 375°F. Season flour with salt and pepper. Cut the cleaned calamari bodies into slices (leave the tentacles whole). Lightly coat calamari with flour mixture, shaking off excess. Fry calamari pieces, a few at a time, for 2 to 3 minutes, until the tentacles have slightly curled and are light golden. Drain on paper towels. Season with Chile-Lime Salt and serve with lime halves.

CHILE-LIME SALT Combine ¼ cup sea salt; 2 fresh red chiles, sliced; and 2 teaspoons lime zest with a mortar and pestle.

FRYING CAN ADD VERY LITTLE FAT WHILE SEALING IN FLAVOR AND MOISTURE TO REACH NEW HEIGHTS OF ENJOYMENT.

PUMPKIN ARANCINI WITH
BLUE CHEESE FONDUE AND PORT WINE SYRUP

serves 4 to 6 • time: 1 hour

Now, I think that calling this a finger food would be selling this dish short. The delicately sweet pumpkin risotto has a simple sophistication that makes it a perfect party dish or appetizer for the most special of occasions.

1   small pumpkin
    Extra-virgin olive oil
    Kosher salt and freshly ground black pepper
¼   cup diced shallots
2   cups Arborio rice
1   cup dry white wine
4   cups reduced-sodium chicken broth, heated
½   stick unsalted butter
½   cup grated Parmigiano-Reggiano
1   cup rice flour
    Fresh Italian flat-leaf parsley leaves, for garnish
1   recipe Blue Cheese Fondue (see recipe, page 141)
1   recipe Port Wine Syrup (see recipe, page 141)

Preheat oven to 350°F. Cut off and discard the top and bottom of the pumpkin. Scoop out and discard the seeds of the pumpkin. Cut off the pumpkin rind; cut pumpkin flesh into large chunks. Drizzle with oil and season with salt and pepper. Roast for 25 to 30 minutes, until tender. Puree flesh in a food processor.

In a large pot heat a 3-count of olive oil (about 3 tablespoons) over medium heat. Add shallots and cook about 5 minutes, until soft. Stir in the rice, making sure to coat all the grains with the oil. Add wine and cook until most of the liquid has evaporated. Ladle in 1 cup of hot broth. Using a wooden spoon, stir gently until most of the stock has been absorbed. Continue adding broth, 1 cup at a time, and stirring. After 10 to 15 minutes, test the rice. It should be cooked and creamy but still have a slight bite to it. (You can add hot water if you use all the broth before the rice is cooked). Stir in butter and Parmigiano-Regianno. Gently fold in roasted pumpkin puree. Season with salt and pepper. Spread the risotto on a large tray; cool in the refrigerator.

Heat a 2-count of olive oil (about 2 tablespoons) in a large heavy pot. To make the arancini, roll risotto into small bite-size balls. Place rice flour on a shallow plate; season with salt and pepper. Dredge balls in seasoned flour. Fry a few at a time for 3 to 4 minutes until golden, adding more oil as necessary. Remove; drain on paper towels. Season with salt. Fry parsley leaves for 15 seconds, until just crispy (be careful; oil may spatter when you add parsley). Garnish arancini with parsley and serve with Blue Cheese Fondue and Port Wine Syrup.

BLUE CHEESE FONDUE In a saucepan heat 2 cups whole milk over medium-high heat until hot. Meanwhile, make a roux by melting 2 tablespoons unsalted butter in a pot over low heat. Stir in 2 tablespoons all-purpose flour until smooth. Add hot milk, 1 cup at a time, whisking constantly to ensure a smooth consistency. Bring to a boil over medium heat; reduce heat. Simmer for 10 minutes. Add ½ teaspoon freshly grated nutmeg and 1 cup crumbled blue cheese; season with kosher salt and freshly ground black pepper. Set aside and keep warm until ready to serve.

PORT WINE SYRUP In a small saucepan heat ½ cup port wine over medium heat. Cook for 5 to 7 minutes until thick and syrupy.

WHILE I LIKE BAR FOOD AS MUCH AS THE NEXT GUY, I HATE TO SEE A GOOD DISH DRAGGED DOWN.

ROSEMARY-GARLIC MOZZARELLA BALLS
WITH ROASTED CHERRY TOMATO DIPPING SAUCE

serves 2 to 4 • time: 45 minutes

I mentioned earlier that frying gets a bad rap, and in a case like fried mozzarella, your local bar is contributing to the damage. But a gorgeous golden brown, savory crust on fresh, creamy mozzarella balls dramatically transforms this bar snack—trust me, you'll never look back.

Mozzarella Balls

- 3 cups cubed focaccia bread
- 4 sprigs fresh rosemary, leaves only
- 2 garlic cloves, peeled and finely shaved
  Kosher salt and freshly ground black pepper
- ½ cup all-purpose flour
- 1 pound buffalo mozzarella, cut into bite-size pieces
- 2 eggs, beaten
  Vegetable oil, for deep-frying

Tomato Dipping Sauce

- 2 cups cherry tomatoes
- ½ medium onion, cut into wedges
- 1 garlic clove, peeled
  Extra-virgin olive oil
  Kosher salt and freshly ground black pepper

To prepare Mozzarella Balls, place bread pieces in a food processor, and pulse until you have about 2 cups coarse bread crumbs. Stir in rosemary leaves and shaved garlic; season with salt and pepper. Place flour on a shallow plate; season with salt and pepper. Dip mozzarella in seasoned flour, shaking off excess. Dip mozzarella into egg, then coat completely in focaccia bread crumbs. Place on a tray; set aside in the refrigerator.

Preheat oven to 425°F. To make Tomato Dipping Sauce, set tomatoes, onion, and garlic on a roasting tray. Drizzle with olive oil and season with salt and pepper. Roast for 15 to 20 minutes, until the tomatoes are slightly caramelized on the top. Remove from oven and transfer to a blender; puree, using a towel to cover the lid and hold down tightly. Transfer tomato mixture to a pot and simmer over low heat until thick and creamy. Season with salt and pepper.

Pour 4 inches oil into a large heavy pot and heat to 375°F. Fry a few mozzarella balls at a time for 3 to 4 minutes, until golden brown and cheese is just beginning to melt. (Keep the oil hot; if the oil cools, the cheese will melt too much and the balls will fall apart.) Drain on paper towels. Season with salt. Serve with Tomato Dipping Sauce.

THE ULTIMATE ONION RINGS | serves 2 to 4 • time: 35 minutes

Somehow the onion ring has followed the career path of the french fry and has branded itself the perfect accoutrement to both the cheap fast food burger and the $40 New York Steak alike. I'm a big onion ring fan and I have been working on this one for a long time—so long that I have given it the "ultimate" moniker. (Yes, they are *that* good.)

2 large onions, sliced ½ inch thick
1 cup all-purpose flour
Kosher salt and freshly ground black pepper
¾ cup all-purpose flour
¼ cup cornstarch
2 tablespoons baking powder
1 teaspoon kosher salt
1 egg yolk
¾ cup club soda, chilled
Vegetable oil, for deep-frying
2 garlic cloves, peeled and shaved
2 tablespoons fresh Italian flat-leaf parsley leaves

Separate onion slices into rings. In a shallow dish, season flour with salt and pepper. Lightly dust onion rings in seasoned flour.

In a large bowl combine the ¾ cup flour, the cornstarch, baking powder, and 1 teaspoon salt. Make a well in the center and add yolk. Gradually whisk in club soda, working your way out from the center to form a smooth batter.

Pour 2 to 3 inches oil into a large heavy pot and heat to 375°F. Dip the flour-coated onion rings into batter, shaking off excess. Fry a few onion rings in oil for 4 to 5 minutes, until golden and puffy. Remove with a slotted spoon; drain on paper towels. Season with salt.

Drop shaved garlic into batter, shake off excess, and fry until golden. Remove with a slotted spoon. Drop parsley leaves in hot oil and fry for 15 seconds, until crispy (be careful; oil may spatter when you add parsley). Remove with a slotted spoon. Sprinkle garlic and parsley on top of fried onion rings.

TEMPURA GREEN BEANS WITH CHILE, GARLIC, AND SESAME AÏOLI

serves 2 to 4 • time: 35 minutes

You've probably seen these in your tempura combo at your favorite sushi spot. Maybe you didn't even notice that they were green beans. Coating crisp, fresh green beans in a traditional Japanese tempura batter creates a uniquely crisp and fluffy texture that differs from everyday battered foods.

Aïoli

- ¼ cup toasted sesame oil
- 2 teaspoons minced ginger
- 2 teaspoons minced garlic
- 1 teaspoon minced red chile
- ½ cup store-bought mayonnaise
- ½ cup sour cream
- 1 teaspoon lemon juice
   Kosher salt and freshly ground black pepper

Tempura Green Beans

- 1 bunch green beans (about 1 pound), root-end trimmed
- ¾ cup all-purpose flour
- ¼ cup cornstarch
- 2 tablespoons baking powder
- 1 teaspoon kosher salt
- 1 egg yolk
- ¾ cup club soda, chilled
   Vegetable oil, for deep-frying
   Kosher salt
- 1 lime, cut into wedges, for garnish
- ¼ bunch fresh cilantro (about 4 sprigs), for garnish

For the Aïoli, heat sesame oil in a small pan over low heat. Add ginger, garlic, and chile and sauté until fragrant and crispy. Drain ginger, garlic, and chile and set aside, reserving the oil.

In a blender combine mayonnaise, sour cream, and the reserved sesame oil. Add lemon juice and season with salt and pepper. Puree until smooth. Set aïoli aside.

For the Tempura Green Beans, in a large bowl combine flour, cornstarch, baking powder, and the 1 teaspoon salt. Make a well in the center and add yolk. Gradually whisk in club soda, slowly working your way out from the center to form a smooth batter.

Pour 2 to 3 inches oil into a large heavy pot and heat to 375°F. Dip green beans into batter, shake off excess, and fry a few at a time for 4 to 5 minutes, until golden and puffy. Drain on paper towels; sprinkle with crispy fried ginger, garlic, and chile. Garnish with lime wedges and cilantro and serve with Aïoli.

TRADITIONAL JAPANESE TEMPURA BATTER CREATES A UNIQUELY CRISP AND FLUFFY TEXTURE THAT DIFFERS FROM EVERYDAY BATTERED FOODS.

GRILL

NOW THAT I LIVE IN CALIFORNIA, I CAN FIRE UP MY OUTDOOR GRILL ABOUT 350 DAYS PER YEAR—IT REALLY ADDS A WHOLE NEW DIMENSION TO PUTTING FOOD ON MY TABLE.

At its core, grilling is open-air cooking with the heat coming from below. Your food sits directly on a hot metal grate that leaves gorgeous marks. Whether you are using gas, charcoal, or wood, successful grilling is all about how you adjust the distance from the food to the heat source and how that affects the balance of getting that brown crust (yup, you know it, COLOR EQUALS FLAVOR) and cooking your food to the desired doneness. If it's too close to the fire, you will scorch the flesh. If you need to control your food's contact with the heat source and your grill doesn't have a vertical adjustment to raise and lower the grate, just think of your grill in terms of zones. Light one side of your grill and leave the other side off. Now you can move your food from one side to the other as you look for more or less heat contact. Another thing to pay attention to is the use of the lid on your grill. Everybody has an opinion on whether or not the lid should be down to speed up the cooking process. There are a few things to consider when making that choice. That's why I'm here. All right everybody, let's get fired up for Grilling 101 …

GRILLED COWBOY RIB-EYE WITH
CREAMED SWISS CHARD AND MEYER LEMON | serves 4 • time: 1 hour

The Cowboy Rib-Eye is the ultimate steak for grilling. With the bone in, it's a big, bold statement on a plate, and you'll want to pick it up and tackle it like Fred Flintstone! A lot of people will tell you that cooking meat on the bone adds flavor, and I'll back that up. The creamed rainbow chard is a great twist on the steak-house staple of creamed spinach. And Jake wouldn't forgive me if I didn't remind you to save the bone for your canine pals…

Extra-virgin olive oil
4 large bone-in rib-eye steaks (16 to 18 ounces each)
Kosher salt and freshly ground black pepper
4 sprigs fresh rosemary
4 sprigs fresh thyme

Creamed Swiss Chard
2 cups heavy whipping cream
3 cloves garlic, peeled and gently smashed
1 large bunch Swiss chard
1 clove garlic, peeled and shaved
2 tablespoons panko bread crumbs
2 Meyer lemons, cut into wedges, to serve

On a large platter drizzle steaks with a 2-count of olive oil (about 2 tablespoons). Season with salt and pepper. Remove the leaves from half of the rosemary and half of the thyme. Sprinkle leaves on steaks; set aside. Preheat grill to medium-high. When the grill is ready, cook the rib-eyes about 7 minutes on each side for medium-rare. (Add another 2 minutes for medium.) Remove from grill and let stand for 5 minutes.

For the Creamed Swiss Chard, while the steaks are cooking heat cream, the remaining thyme and rosemary sprigs, and the 3 cloves garlic in a large saucepan over medium heat. Simmer until mixture is slightly reduced. Strain the cream mixture and return to saucepan.

Preheat broiler. Split each Swiss chard leaf lengthwise so each piece has a bit of stem and a bit of leaf. In a large pot of boiling salted water, blanch leaves until wilted; drain and squeeze dry to remove as much moisture as possible. Fold the Swiss chard into the strained cream. Warm over low heat and season to taste with salt and pepper. Transfer chard to individual ovenproof dishes; top with the 1 clove shaved garlic and the panko crumbs. Broil until crispy and golden, about 3 minutes. Serve grilled rib-eyes with Creamed Swiss Chard and Meyer lemon wedges.

FOOD SITS DIRECTLY ON A METAL GRATE THAT LEAVES GORGEOUS MARKS, SENDING A MESSAGE TO EVERYBODY THAT YOU ARE A TRUE GRILL MASTER.

STEAK AND BACON BLUE CHEESE WEDGE | serves 4 • time: 30 minutes

Any great steak house has that most masculine of salads, the wedge, on the menu.
But why bother with side dishes when you throw the steak and bacon right in the salad!

Extra-virgin olive oil, plus more for drizzling
1   2-pound beef tenderloin
Kosher salt and freshly ground black pepper
8   slices bacon
6   medium heirloom tomatoes, cut into 6 wedges

Creamy Dressing
1   cup store-bought mayonnaise
1   cup sour cream
6   ounces crumbled mild blue cheese (¾ cup)
1   tablespoon lemon juice
2   tablespoons chopped chives
Kosher salt and freshly ground black pepper

2   romaine lettuce hearts, halved lengthwise
½   loaf French bread, cut into ¼-inch cubes
1   recipe Crispy Potato Cakes (see recipe, page 153)
1   recipe Arugula Pesto (see recipe, page 171)

Preheat grill to high. Rub oil all over the tenderloin; season generously
with salt and pepper. Place tenderloin on hot grill and cook about
4 minutes on each side so it sears evenly (16 minutes total), or until the
tenderloin is cooked medium-rare. (Add another 4 minutes for medium).
Let stand for 5 minutes on a plate tented with foil before slicing.

Meanwhile, preheat oven to 375°F. On a roasting tray, lay the bacon
flat and cook for 7 to 8 minutes, until crispy. Drain on paper towels;
set aside. In a bowl drizzle tomato wedges with oil and season with
salt and pepper.

For the Creamy Dressing, in a large bowl combine the mayonnaise,
sour cream, blue cheese, lemon juice, and chives. Stir with a whisk
until everything is combined. The dressing should remain slightly
chunky because of the blue cheese. (The dressing can be made ahead
of time and refrigerated until ready to serve.)

Serve tenderloin slices with tomato wedges, romaine, bacon slices,
and bread cubes. Drizzle with Creamy Dressing. Serve with Crispy
Potato Cakes and Arugula Pesto.

CRISPY POTATO CAKES Peel 4 medium Yukon gold potatoes; cut into shreds, using a mandoline or grater. Place shreds in a kitchen towel and squeeze out moisture. In a large bowl combine potatoes with ¼ cup chopped onion, 2 egg whites, and 2 tablespoons rice flour (or all-purpose flour, if rice flour can't be found). Season with kosher salt and freshly ground black pepper. In a large nonstick sauté pan heat a 3-count of extra-virgin olive oil (about 3 tablespoons) over medium heat. Drop potato mixture in 1-tablespoon portions in the pan, gently pressing down to form a round cake. Fry for 5 to 7 minutes per side, until golden brown and crispy. Drain on paper towels; season with salt.

LAMB T-BONES WITH
SMASHED POTATOES AND PEAS | serves 4 to 6 • time: 1 hour 30 minutes *(includes marinating)*

The lamb T-bone is the equivalent of a porterhouse. You get a little bit of the strip on one side and tenderloin on the other. The tenderest chop available, it's great for throwing right on the grill, and cooking on the bone always adds the most flavor. The bright flavor of the lemon parsley sauce highlights the delicate flavor of the lamb. I just love pairing it with the comfortable, warm combination of potatoes and peas.

8   4-ounce lamb T-bone loin chops (about 2 pounds total)
1   lemon, juice only
1   bay leaf
1   shallot, roughly chopped
¼   cup fresh Italian flat-leaf parsley, roughly chopped
    Extra-virgin olive oil
    Kosher salt and freshly ground black pepper
    Fresh mint leaves

Smashed Potatoes and Peas
8   medium new baby red potatoes
½   cup heavy whipping cream
    Extra-virgin olive oil
1   cup frozen peas, blanched*
4   sprigs fresh mint, leaves only
    Kosher salt and freshly ground black pepper

In a large bowl combine lamb with lemon juice, bay leaf, shallot, parsley, and a 2-count of olive oil (about 2 tablespoons). Season with salt and pepper Cover the bowl with plastic wrap and marinate in the refrigerator for 45 minutes. Preheat the grill to high. Quickly and carefully wipe the grate with oiled paper towels to create a nonstick surface. Grill chops about 2 minutes per side for medium-rare (130°F). Let stand for 5 minutes before serving. Garnish with mint leaves.

Meanwhile, for the Smashed Potatoes and Peas, place potatoes in a large pot of cold salted water. Bring to a boil, then simmer for 20 to 30 minutes or until potatoes are fork-tender. Drain and return to the pot. Add cream and a drizzle of oil. Smash the potatoes with a wooden spoon to break them up a little and incorporate the cream. Fold in peas and mint. Season with salt and pepper.

*TIP To blanch the peas, submerge them in boiling water for 1 minute, drain them, and plunge them into ice water to stop the cooking process. Drain them again and set aside.

CHICKEN SPIEDINI SALAD | serves 4 • time: 45 minutes

"Spiedini" is an Italian word used for anything that you cook on a stick. When I was touring Italy, I found beautiful meat and seafood grilled in this way everywhere I went, and it inspired me to create this dish.

Spiedini

1	crusty baguette, sliced into rounds
2	medium boneless, skin-on chicken breast halves, cut into 4 pieces each
4	links sweet Italian pork sausage, halved crosswise
12	fresh bay leaves
½	cup extra-virgin olive oil
	Kosher salt and freshly ground black pepper
2	lemons, juice only

Salad

2	anchovy fillets
1	clove garlic, peeled
1	tablespoon lemon juice
2	egg yolks
2	tablespoons water
1	cup extra-virgin olive oil
2	tablespoons grated Parmigiano-Reggiano
	Kosher salt and freshly ground black pepper
2	heads romaine lettuce, cut into 6 wedges through the stem
2	lemons, halved and grilled
	Finely shredded Parmigiano-Reggiano

Using four metal skewers, thread the components, alternating bread, chicken, sausage, and bay leaves, until the skewers are full. Baste the kabobs with the ½ cup olive oil; season with salt and pepper. Preheat grill to medium. Place kabobs on the hot grill; turn heat to medium. Cook for 8 to 10, until golden brown, basting with lemon juice and turning to ensure even color on all asides.

Meanwhile, prepare the salad. Combine the anchovies, garlic, lemon juice, and egg yolks in a blender. Blend to combine; add the water and blend again. With the blender running, slowly pour the 1 cup oil through the hole in the top; blend until emulsified (thickened). Add the 2 tablespoons Parmigiano-Reggiano; blend just to combine. Season to taste with salt and pepper. Place the romaine in a large bowl. Add some dressing and gently toss to combine. When the kabobs are done, remove from the grill. Serve kabobs with romaine and grilled lemons and sprinkle with shredded Parmigiano-Reggiano.

"SPIEDINI" IS AN ITALIAN WORD USED FOR ANYTHING THAT YOU COOK ON A STICK.

GRILLED TURKEY WITH CELERY-WALNUT PESTO AND CRISPY FINGERLING POTATOES

serves 8 to 10 • time: 2 hours

Believe it or not, you are allowed to cook turkey all year-round, not just in November. Throw these pieces on the grill, and you will wonder why you ever tried to stuff that 20-pound bird into your oven!

Celery-Walnut Pesto

1   cup unsalted walnuts
½   cup pine nuts
    Kosher salt and freshly ground black pepper
2   garlic cloves, peeled
1   cup fresh Italian flat-leaf parsley
2   cups celery leaves
1   teaspoon lemon juice
½   cup grated Parmigiano-Reggiano
¾   cup extra-virgin olive oil

Grilled Turkey

1   12- to 14-pound fresh turkey (have a butcher cut it into
        4 pieces and remove bones from breast)
    Extra-virgin olive oil
1   lemon, juice only
    Kosher salt and freshly ground black pepper

Crispy Fingerling Potatoes

1   pound fingerling potatoes, cut into ¼-inch slices
    Extra-virgin olive oil
    Kosher salt and freshly ground black pepper

Preheat oven to 350°F. For the Celery-Walnut Pesto, arrange the walnuts and pine nuts on separate ends of a baking sheet and toast for 8 to 10 minutes, until golden brown, stirring once. Season walnuts immediately with salt, then set both nuts aside to cool. Combine cooled walnuts and pine nuts, garlic, parsley, celery leaves, lemon juice, and Parmigiano-Reggiano in a food processor; pulse to combine. Drizzle the ¾ cup oil into the processer and blend until the mixture is combined but still has texture. Season with salt and pepper.

Drizzle the 4 turkey pieces lightly with oil and lemon juice. Season with salt and pepper. Preheat the grill to medium. Quickly and carefully wipe the grate with oiled paper towels to create a nonstick surface. Put the turkey pieces on the grill, skin sides down, and cook, uncovered, for 30 minutes. Turn the pieces over and baste with more oil. Continue grilling about 30 minutes more, until the juices run clear (180°F in the thigh). Set aside, cover with foil, and let stand about 10 minutes.

About 40 minutes before the turkey is done, preheat oven to 350°F. Toss potato slices in oil and season with salt and pepper. Place potatoes on a roasting tray and roast for 25 to 30 minutes until golden and crispy.

To serve, place turkey pieces and potatoes on a large platter. Spread the Celery-Walnut Pesto over the turkey.

CITRUS-GLAZED QUAIL WITH ROASTED PEACHES, POLENTA, AND BITTER GREENS

serves 4 • time: 1 hour

You don't find quail at many backyard barbecues, but don't be intimidated. These flavorful little birds require a real hands-on approach to eating, but it's well worth getting your fingers a little bit sticky. The citrus glaze is the perfect complement to these birds and the smooth, creamy potato puree rounds out the bitterness of the greens to complete this unique dish.

3 blood oranges, juice only
¼ cup peach nectar
8 3-ounce semi-boneless quail
Extra-virgin olive oil
Kosher salt and freshly ground black pepper
4 peaches
1 recipe Polenta (see recipe, below)
1 bunch bitter greens, for garnish

For the glaze, in a small saucepan heat the blood orange juice and peach nectar and set over medium heat. Simmer for 4 to 5 minutes, until reduced and slightly syrupy. Set aside.

Wash quail under cold running water and pat dry with paper towels. Rub birds with a little oil and season inside cavities and outsides of birds with salt and pepper. Preheat grill to medium. Grill birds for 6 to 8 minutes per side (12 to 16 minutes total), basting with glaze with a small pastry brush, until skin is golden and crispy.

Meanwhile, split peaches and remove stones. Drizzle peach halves with oil and season with salt and pepper. Grill peaches for 2 to 3 minutes per side, until grill marks appear, then set aside.

Serve quail on Polenta with grilled peaches. Garnish with greens

POLENTA In a large saucepan combine 1½ quarts chicken broth with ¾ teaspoon kosher salt; bring to a boil. Gradually pour in 1½ cups polenta or yellow cornmeal in a slow, steady stream, whisking constantly. Once the broth is completely absorbed, lower the heat and continue cooking for 20 minutes, whisking often. (The polenta should be thick and smooth.) Add ¼ cup heavy whipping cream and 1½ tablespoons unsalted butter; cook another 10 minutes, whisking often. Stir in ¾ cup grated Parmigiano-Reggiano and season with freshly ground black pepper.

GRILLED TUNA WITH WHITE BEAN PUREE, OLIVE TAPENADE, AND ROASTED CHERRY TOMATOES

serves 2 to 4 • time: 50 minutes

I love this Mediterranean take on the grilled tuna steak. The gorgeous grill marks contrast with the moist, rare flesh of the fish. The creamy white bean puree and the tapenade offer two totally different dimensions to the dish—which I find myself going back and forth between them.

1 pint on-the-vine cherry tomatoes
½ cup Orange-Chile Oil (see recipe, page 163)

Olive Tapenade
1 cup pitted kalamata olives
1 small garlic clove, peeled
   Pinch crushed red pepper flakes
4 sprigs fresh Italian flat-leaf parsley
1 tablespoon fresh tarragon
1 tablespoon red or white wine vinegar
3 tablespoons extra-virgin olive oil
   Kosher salt and freshly ground black pepper

White Bean Puree
   Extra-virgin olive oil
2 garlic cloves, peeled and roughly chopped
2 anchovy flllets
2 14-ounce cans white cannellini beans, drained
½ cup chicken broth, heated
2 teaspoons white wine vinegar
   Kosher salt and freshly ground black pepper

Tuna
2 sushi-quality tuna steaks (such as Ahi), about 1 inch thick
     (6 to 8 ounces each)
   Extra-virgin olive oil
   Kosher salt and freshly ground black pepper
   Israeli arugula (or regular arugula)

Preheat oven to 375°F. Lay tomatoes in a single layer on a roasting tray. Drizzle with Orange-Chile Oil. Roast tomatoes for 8 to 10 minutes, until tomatoes burst and give off their juices.

To prepare the tapenade, combine olives, garlic, red pepper flakes, parsley, tarragon, vinegar, and oil in a food processor. Pulse until a coarse puree forms. Adjust seasoning with salt and pepper; set aside.

For the White Bean Puree, place a saucepan over medium heat and add a 2-count of oil (about 2 tablespoons). Add the garlic and anchovies and cook until garlic is fragrant. Add the drained beans and

warm broth; cook until heated through. Transfer the mixture to a clean food processor; add vinegar and puree. (Thin with extra broth if the puree is too thick.) Season to taste with salt and pepper. Set aside and keep warm until ready to serve.

Heat the grill to high. Drizzle the tuna with oil and season with salt and pepper. Place tuna on the hot grill; cook about 45 seconds. Turn tuna and cook for another 45 seconds. (The tuna should be rare on the inside and have nice grill marks on the outside.) Serve tuna with Olive Tapenade, White Bean Puree, arugula, and roasted on-the-vine tomatoes.

ORANGE-CHILE OIL In a bowl combine 4 sprigs fresh thyme, 2 fresh rosemary sprigs, 1½ tablespoons crushed red pepper flakes, 2 strips orange peel, and 1½ cups extra-virgin olive oil. Set aside for at least 1 hour to let the flavors infuse. Cover and store remaining oil in the refrigerator for 2 to 3 months.

THE ULTIMATE SHRIMP AND GRITS | serves 4 to 6 • time: 45 minutes

There are more variations of shrimp and grits than you can shake a stick at, but I think this one works perfectly. The clean grilled flavor of the shrimp shines through the gravy and creamy grits.

Grits

1½ cups milk, plus a splash
1½ cups heavy whipping cream
 1 cup stone-ground white cornmeal
 1 tablespoon unsalted butter
   Kosher salt and freshly ground black pepper

   Extra-virgin olive oil
 1 medium white onion, minced
 1 garlic clove, peeled and minced
 1 pound spicy andouille sausage links, cut into bite-size pieces
 2 tablespoons all-purpose flour
 2 cups chicken broth
 1 bay leaf
 2 pounds large shrimp, peeled and deveined, tails on
   Kosher salt and freshly ground black pepper
   Pinch cayenne pepper
 4 shakes bottled hot sauce
 ½ lemon, juice only
 2 tablespoons finely chopped fresh Italian flat-leaf parsley
 2 tablespoons finely chopped chives

 1 recipe Buttermilk Biscuits (see recipe, page 165)

To make the grits, place a 3-quart pot over medium-high heat and add the milk and cream. Bring to a simmer. Slowly add the cornmeal, whisking constantly. When the grits begin to bubble, reduce the heat and simmer, stirring frequently with a wooden spoon. Cook for 10 to 15 minutes, until the mixture is smooth and thick. Remove from heat, and stir in the butter. (Thin grits with a little extra cream, if necessary). Season with salt and pepper.

To make the sauce, in a deep skillet heat a 2-count of olive oil (about 2 tablespoons) over medium heat. Add the white onion and garlic; sauté for 2 minutes to soften. Add the sausage and cook, stirring, until a fair amount of fat has rendered and the sausage is brown. Sprinkle the flour into the fat and stir to create a roux. Slowly pour in the broth, continue stirring to avoid lumps. Add the bay leaf. When the liquid comes to a simmer, remove from heat. Keep warm.

THERE ARE MORE VARIATIONS OF SHRIMP AND GRITS THAN YOU CAN SHAKE A STICK AT.

Preheat the grill to medium-high. Quickly and carefully wipe the grate with oiled paper towels to create a nonstick surface. Season shrimp with plenty of salt and pepper. Place shrimp on grill; cook for 1 to 2 minutes per side until shrimp turn pink. Fold the grilled shrimp into the sauce. Add the cayenne pepper, hot sauce, and lemon juice. Season with salt and pepper. Stir in the parsley and chives. Serve shrimp on top of the grits with Buttermilk Biscuits.

BUTTERMILK BISCUITS Preheat the oven to 375°F. In a large bowl sift together the 4 cups all-purpose flour, 1 tablespoon salt, 1 tablespoon baking powder, and 2 teaspoons baking soda. Cut 1 cup of cold shortening into ½-inch pieces. Using a pastry blender or your hands, cut in the pieces of shortening until the mixture resembles coarse crumbs. Make a well in the center of the flour mixture and add 1 cup buttermilk. Using your hands, quickly fold the dry ingredients into the buttermilk until a sticky dough forms. (If the dough is too dry, you can add ½ to 1 cup of additional buttermilk, a little at a time, until a sticky dough forms.) Turn the dough out onto a floured surface. Gently fold the dough three or four times to create layers. Press the dough out to a 1½-inch thickness and cut with a floured 3-inch biscuit cutter. Lay the biscuits on an ungreased cookie sheet and brush the tops with additional buttermilk. Bake for 20 to 25 minutes, until golden brown. Makes 9 biscuits.

HOG ISLAND OYSTERS CASINO | serves 4 to 6 • time: 25 minutes

Just up the coast from San Francisco is the Hog Island Oyster Company, where I get the most delicious, sustainably raised shellfish I can find. You can grill your oysters right there at the farm or take them home. I love oysters right out of the water in their natural state, but sometimes it's nice to give them a little something extra. A little bacon, butter, onion, lemon … wow. Throw them on the grill and add your Casino mixture right on top of the half shell. That's what I'm talking about.

1 stick unsalted butter, room temperature
2 garlic cloves, peeled and minced
4 slices bacon
¼ cup roughly chopped shallots
¼ cup roughly chopped red bell pepper
¼ cup roughly chopped celery
2 teaspoons lemon juice
2 sprigs fresh oregano, leaves only
Pinch cayenne pepper
Kosher salt and freshly ground black pepper
2 dozen medium-size (4-inch diameter) West Coast oysters
on the half shell
4 sprigs fresh Italian flat-leaf parsley, finely chopped, for garnish

In a food processor combine the butter, garlic, bacon, shallots, bell pepper, celery, lemon juice, oregano, and cayenne pepper; pulse until consistent, but still has texture. Season with salt and black pepper to taste.

Preheat the grill to high. Place 1 tablespoon of the butter mixture on top of each oyster. Grill oysters for 10 to 12 minutes, until bubbly. Sprinkle with parsley and serve.

THERE IS SOMETHING TOTALLY MACHO ABOUT COOKING OVER AN OPEN FLAME.

GRILLED FLAT BREAD WITH CARAMELIZED ONIONS, GORGONZOLA MASCARPONE, AND CRUNCHY RED GRAPES

serves 4 to 6 • time: 35 minutes

If your friends and family like pizza—and who doesn't—try this grill-friendly recipe. The inspiration for this one came while I was in Florence shooting *Tyler's Ultimate* a couple of years ago. No tomato sauce, just the crispy grilled bread, soft white mascarpone, sweet grapes, and caramelized onions. This one has a truly unique flavor profile.

Extra-virgin olive oil
3 large onions, sliced
1 large store-bought rustic-style flat bread
Kosher salt and freshly ground black pepper
2 cups mascarpone
1 cup crumbled Gorgonzola
1 cup toasted walnuts, roughly chopped
2 cups firm red grapes, halved
2 tablespoons chopped fresh Italian flat-leaf parsley

In a large sauté pan heat a 2-count of olive oil (about 2 tablespoons) over medium heat. Add onions and slowly caramelize until brown and creamy. Set aside.

Preheat the grill to high. Quickly and carefully wipe the grate with oiled paper towels to create a nonstick surface. Brush the flat bread with oil and season with salt and pepper. Reduce grill heat to medium. Grill bread on both sides until warmed through and brown with grill marks.

Quickly transfer flat bread to a platter and smear with mascarpone while still warm. Sprinkle with Gorgonzola, caramelized onions, toasted walnuts, and grapes. Season with a few turns of freshly ground black pepper, drizzle lightly with some additional oil, and top with a shower of fresh parsley.

GRILLED BRIE AND TOMATO ON CRUSTY BREAD | serves 4 • time: 15 minutes

A good, crusty slice of bread grills up just as well as anything else and really picks up nice color and texture. The grilled tomatoes seem to melt just like the creamy Brie and the soft toppings really work on top that warm, crunchy bread. Fire up this toasted bread for those who don't eat meat in your group or put it on the fire right alongside your favorite meats.

Arugula Pesto

- 4 cups arugula
- 1 cup fresh basil leaves
- 2 garlic cloves, peeled
- ¼ cup pine nuts, toasted
- ½ cup extra-virgin olive oil
  Kosher salt and freshly ground black pepper

- 1 baguette, thick bias-cut slices
  Extra-virgin olive oil
- 4 ripe tomatoes, sliced
- ½ pound Brie, sliced thin

For the Arugula Pesto, in a food processor combine arugula, basil, garlic, and pine nuts and process until mixture becomes a smooth puree. With the motor running, slowly pour the ½ cup oil through the food tube until you get a spreadable consistency. Season with salt and pepper.

Preheat grill to medium. Drizzle the bread slices with oil, then grill about 1 minute per side. Remove bread from grill. Spread each slice with some of the pesto. Add a layer of sliced tomato and a piece of Brie. Grill about 1 minute more, until cheese melts and the bread is nicely toasted.

A GOOD, CRUSTY SLICE OF BREAD GRILLS UP JUST AS WELL AS ANYTHING ELSE.

STEAM

LISTEN, I CARE ABOUT BEING HEALTHY AS MUCH AS THE NEXT GUY. BUT THIS IS A COOKBOOK, NOT A DIET MANUAL. THAT'S NOT TO SAY I DON'T TAKE IT ALL INTO CONSIDERATION WHEN WRITING THESE RECIPES, BUT SOMETIMES CERTAIN RECIPES AND STYLES OF COOKING DEMAND A BIT OF FAT.

But here—with steaming—we have the opportunity to explore some lighter and inherently more healthful cooking that I know you will love. Steaming, believe it or not, is actually a beautifully delicate cooking technique that deserves some real attention. Sometimes I feel like dieters look to steamed items as a means of cutting out all of the good stuff. But there's a lot more to it. Steaming is actually something to be excited about, not a death sentence for your taste buds.

Steaming takes place when your food is cooked by the water in the form of gas. Essentially, boiling water turns into steam, and that steam heats your food. The moisture that cooks out of your food then drops back down into the water. It's pretty simple, really, and a great way to cook with no fat at all. You can achieve some pretty amazing results with lighter, faster fare—think vegetables and seafood. HERE, COLOR DOES NOT EQUAL FLAVOR, so let's consider adding a bit of flavor to your steam with some herbs, broth, or wine. But keep in mind that you still need a high water content to keep that steam coming. Steaming is more than just a way to cook without fat. It's a way to showcase the beautifully delicate flavors and textures of some lighter foods, and it's time we all started to explore steaming so we can add it to our everyday repertoire. So here we go. One, two, three … steam!

PORK AND RICE CABBAGE
WRAPS WITH CELLOPHANE NOODLES

serves 4 • time: 1 hour

Between New York City and San Francisco, I've spent a lot of time eating and shopping my way through Chinatown. Steamed cabbage wraps are always at the top of my list when I'm exploring Asian flavors. I love how the steaming allows the spices to shine through, unhindered by starches or oils.

Shiitake Broth

1½	quarts reduced-sodium chicken broth
2	green onions, sliced
1	fresh red chile, sliced
1	1-inch piece of ginger, peeled
2	tablespoons toasted sesame oil
2	tablespoons soy sauce
4	shiitake mushrooms

Cabbage Wraps

1	napa cabbage
1	pound ground pork
2	egg yolks
1	tablespoon minced ginger
1	garlic clove, peeled and minced
¼	teaspoon minced fresh red chile
2	teaspoons toasted sesame oil
1	tablespoon soy sauce
1½	cups steamed jasmine rice

16	ounces cellophane rice noodles
	Fresh cilantro, for garnish

To prepare the Shiitake Broth, in a large pot combine broth, green onions, red chile, ginger, oil, soy sauce, and shiitake mushrooms over medium heat. Bring to a boil, then reduce heat and simmer while you prepare the wraps.

To make the Cabbage Wraps, separate cabbage leaves. Prepare a bowl of ice water, for plunging the leaves in when they come out of the hot water. Place a few cabbage leaves at a time in a large pot of boiling salted water and cook for about 1 minute. Remove leaves from water with tongs; immediately plunge them into the ice water to stop the cooking process and keep the leaves green. Dry leaves with paper towels. In a large bowl combine pork, yolks, ginger, garlic, chile, oil, soy sauce, and rice; mix well to combine. Take one cabbage leaf at a time and place about 1 tablespoon of the pork mixture on one end. Roll it up, folding in the sides as you go; set aside, seam-side down. Continue until you run out of mixture. Strain broth, discarding green onions and

ginger. Slice red chile and mushrooms and fold back into the broth. Cook the noodles in the broth for 5 to 7 minutes, then drain, reserving broth, and divide among bowls. Return broth to pot over medium heat. Carefully drop cabbage wraps in the broth, seam-side down. Cover and gently simmer for 10 minutes. Serve with the noodles and hot broth. Garnish with fresh cilantro.

WEST COAST CIOPPINO | serves 4 to 6 • time: 1 hour 30 minutes

An Italian classic? Not quite. Cioppino is a true San Francisco original. According to local legend, in the late 1800s, Italian fisherman ruled Fisherman's Wharf and every day one fisherman went from boat to boat asking his buddies to "Chip in! Chip in!" to his pot of seafood for a stew for them all to share. Well, say it out loud with a heavy Italian accent and, so they say, "Chip-een-o" was born. This story may not hold water, but one thing is for sure: This delicious catch-of-the-day chowder is savory, aromatic, and a real showcase of the sea's bounty. And, of course, San Francisco sourdough bread is a natural fit.

Cioppino

- 1 pound Spanish chorizo links
  Extra-virgin olive oil
- 1 28-ounce can whole San Marzano tomatoes
- 1 large onion
- 2 garlic cloves, peeled
- 2 ribs celery
- 4 sprigs fresh thyme
- 1 bay leaf
- ¼ cup all-purpose flour
- 1 cup dry red wine
- 2 cups low-sodium chicken broth
  Kosher salt and freshly ground black pepper
- 2 fresh Dungeness crabs (2 pounds each), cut into 6 pieces
- 16 littleneck clams, cleaned and scrubbed
- 16 large uncooked shrimp, peeled and deveined
- 4 halibut fillets (about 8 ounces each)
- 1 lemon, halved, to serve
- 4 sprigs fresh Italian flat-leaf parsley, chopped, for garnish
- 1 recipe Sourdough Garlic Toasts (see recipe, page 177)

Place the chorizo in a food processor and process until the pieces are small and well ground. In a Dutch oven or large heavy pot heat a 2-count of olive oil (about 2 tablespoons) over medium heat; cook the ground chorizo until brown and the fat is rendered. Meanwhile, drain the tomatoes, reserving the juice. Hand-crush the tomatoes. Add the onion, garlic, celery, and hand-crushed tomatoes to the food processor and process until a smooth, slightly pulpy consistency is reached.

Once the ground chorizo is cooked, add the vegetable puree, the thyme, and bay leaf to the pot and sauté for 5 to 7 minutes more. When the liquid has reduced a little, dust with the flour and stir well to form the base of a roux. Add the reserved tomato juice, the red wine, and chicken broth. Season lightly with salt and pepper, then cover (leaving lid slightly askew) and simmer for 1 hour.

Turn up the heat and add the crabs and clams to the broth. Cover and steam about 10 minutes, until clams open. Discard any that don't open. Reduce heat; add shrimp, halibut, and lemon; gently mix to coat everything. Simmer gently until shrimp turn pink and fish is cooked through; remove from heat. Serve Cioppino with Sourdough Garlic Toasts and top with a spoonful of reserved garlic butter and some fresh parsley.

SOURDOUGH GARLIC TOASTS Preheat oven to 350°F. In a bowl combine ½ stick room-temperature unsalted butter; 2 garlic cloves, peeled and minced; and 2 tablespoons chopped fresh Italian flat-leaf parsley; stir to mix. Season with kosher salt and freshly ground black pepper. Cut 1 loaf of sourdough bread into slices, leaving them connected at the base so the bread is still in a loaf. Smear the insides of the bread slices with some of the garlic butter (set aside remaining butter for Cioppino). Place loaf on a baking sheet. Toast the whole loaf about 10 minutes, until crispy and fragrant. Top servings of the Cioppino with leftover garlic butter.

SEA BASS WITH HERBS AND LEMON EN PAPILLOTE | serves 2 to 4 • time: 40 minutes

It has been said that the true test of a Chinese chef is his whole steamed fish. You can't hide a second-rate fish with this technique, as it is all right there in front of you, free of sauce and spices. The herbs and lemon are a natural complement to the firm white sea bass flesh, which remains moist and tender.

1 2-pound whole sea bass, cleaned and scaled
  Kosher salt and freshly ground black pepper
2 tablespoons fresh parsley, roughly chopped
2 teaspoons fresh oregano, roughly chopped
1 sprig fresh thyme, leaves only
1 lemon, finely sliced
⅓ cup dry white wine
  Extra-virgin olive oil
  Lemon wedges, to serve

Preheat oven to 425°F. Tear off a sheet of parchment paper in the shape of a rectangle that is twice the size of your fish, with about 2 inches to spare all the way around. Set the paper on a roasting pan, then lay the fish on one half of the paper. Using a sharp knife, make cuts on the fish so it will cook evenly. Season the inside and outside of the fish with salt and pepper, then stuff the herbs and lemon inside the cavity. Pour wine over the fish and drizzle with oil.

Fold the paper over onto itself to envelop the fish and, working from one corner around to the other, fold over the edges to create an almost airtight seal. Brush the top of the paper with oil. Bake for 20 to 25 minutes. When done, the paper will puff like a balloon. Cut the paper open at the table for a dramatic presentation and finish with a squeeze of lemon juice and a drizzle of oil.

STEAMING IS SOMETHING TO BE EXCITED ABOUT, NOT A DEATH SENTENCE FOR YOUR TASTE BUDS.

STEAMED SHRIMP WITH
LAGER, LEMON, AND THYME

serves 2 to 4 • time: 25 minutes

Bring out the natural sweetness of shrimp by steaming them in a flavorful brew of lager, lemon, and thyme. The broth infuses the shrimp with a nice flavor and the aroma is out of this world. Don't worry, the alcohol cooks out as the liquid turns to gas so you'll be okay to drive home.

- 4 12-ounce bottles lager
- 1 tablespoon cider vinegar
- ½ lemon
- 1 garlic head, split in half through the equator (horizontally)
- 3 bay leaves
- 2 sprigs fresh thyme
- 1½ teaspoons black mustard seeds
- 2 dried red chiles
- 1 tablespoon Old Bay seasoning
- 1 teaspoon sugar
- 2 pounds large shrimp, heads and tails on

For the court-bouillon, combine all the ingredients, except the shrimp, in a large stockpot and place over high heat. Bring to a boil, then reduce heat and simmer for 10 minutes to allow the flavors to come together. Add shrimp and return to a boil. Immediately shut off the heat, cover the pot, and let the shrimp steam in the court-bouillon for 12 to 15 minutes, until they turn pink. Strain and serve.

YOU CAN ACHIEVE SOME PRETTY AMAZING RESULTS WITH LIGHTER, FASTER FARE—THINK VEGETABLES AND SEAFOOD.

SALMON MOUSSE WITH PICKLED RED ONIONS AND CUCUMBERS

serves 4 to 6 • time: 1 hour

Here's an interesting way to treat salmon—and a great appetizer for your next party. Steaming the fish leaves the flesh pristinely pink and moist, a perfect starting point for the mousse.

Salmon Mousse

- ⅔ pound fresh salmon fillet
- ⅓ pound smoked salmon
- 5 egg yolks
- 2 tablespoons crème fraîche
  Kosher salt
- 2 cups heavy whipping cream

Pickled Red Onions and Cucumbers

- ¼ cup red wine vinegar
- 2 tablespoons sugar
- 1 small red onion, very thinly sliced
- 1 hothouse English cucumber
- 2 tablespoons fresh Italian flat-leaf parsley

- ½ baguette, sliced and toasted

Preheat oven to 250°F. Remove skin from salmon. Cut both kinds of salmon into large cubes. Combine salmon, yolks, and crème fraîche in a food processor. Season with salt. With the motor running, pour the cream through the feed tube until you have a smooth paste that is light and airy. Divide salmon among four 6-ounce ramekins; place ramekins in a large roasting pan and fill pan with hot water about halfway up the sides of the ramekins. Cover the pan with aluminum foil and bake for 30 to 35 minutes until mousse springs back slightly when touched. Remove ramekins from water bath and cool on a wire rack for 10 minutes before placing in the refrigerator to chill for 30 minutes.

For the Pickled Onions and Cucumber, combine vinegar and sugar in a bowl until sugar has completely dissolved. Add onion and cucumbers. Cover and refrigerate for 15 minutes before serving. Drain and toss with parsley.

Serve mousse with Pickled Onions and Cucumbers and crispy toasted slices of baguette.

CLAMS WITH CHORIZO, CITRUS, AND SAFFRON AÏOLI

serves 4 • time: 45 minutes

Clams are relatively small, delicate creatures and can turn into tough shriveled raisins if you overcook them. Steaming them cooks them through yet keeps them plump and juicy. I love throwing a Spanish twist into the mix with the spicy chorizo and a hint of saffron.

¾ pound Spanish chorizo
   Extra-virgin olive oil
2 garlic cloves, peeled and minced
2 slices orange
2 dozen littleneck clams
½ cup Albariño wine or dry white wine
   Kosher salt and freshly ground black pepper
   Fresh Italian flat-leaf parsley, for garnish
1 recipe Saffron Aïoli (see recipe, below)

Rinse the clams under running water and scrub with a brush; set aside. Place the chorizo in a food processor and process until the pieces are small and well ground. In a large heavy pot heat a 2-count of olive oil (about 2 tablespoons) over medium heat. Add garlic and orange slices; add ground chorizo. Gently sauté until fragrant and fat begins to render. Add clams and wine. Season with salt and pepper. Cover and steam for 12 to 15 minutes, until clams open. Discard any that don't open. Remove lid and spoon ¼ cup Saffron Aïoli over the top; toss to combine and coat the clams. Serve in a large bowl garnished with parsley.

SAFFRON AÏOLI Combine ½ teaspoon saffron threads and 1 tablespoon warm water. Soak for several minutes. In a blender combine saffron, water, 3 egg yolks, ½ cup blanched slivered almonds, 3 tablespoons Spanish paprika, and the juice of ½ lemon; blend until combined. With the blender running, slowly pour in 1 cup extra-virgin olive oil in a slow and steady stream so the aïoli emulsifies. Season with kosher salt and freshly ground black pepper. Spoon aïoli into a bowl. Finish by adding a drizzle of olive oil. Refrigerate until ready to use.

STEAMING IS ACTUALLY A BEAUTIFUL, DELICATE COOKING TECHNIQUE THAT DESERVES SOME REAL ATTENTION.

MUSSELS WITH
COCONUT GREEN CURRY AND LIME

serves 2 to 4 • time: 35 minutes

Humans have been eating mussels for at least 200,000 years, so they must be good. They are a bit tougher than clams, and steaming is the way to go to keep them plump and juicy. Before you start cooking, throw out any mussels that appear broken or that won't close when tapped. After you've steamed them, toss any that won't open. The sweetness of mussels really stands out with this green curry and its burst of lime.

- 3 pounds mussels
- 2 tablespoons Thai green curry paste
- ½ lime, juice only
- 1 cup chopped fresh cilantro
- 1 15-ounce can coconut milk
  Vegetable oil, for shallow frying
- ¼ cup all-purpose flour
  Kosher salt
- 2 shallots, finely sliced
- 2 limes, cut into wedges, for garnish
  Fresh cilantro, for garnish

Rinse the mussels under cold running water and scrub with a brush. Remove the stringy mussel beards with your thumb and index finger as you wash them. Discard any mussels with broken shells.

Combine curry paste, lime juice, the 1 cup chopped cilantro, and 2 tablespoons of the coconut milk in a blender. Blend until smooth and bright green; set aside.

In a large pot over high heat add the mussels and the remaining coconut milk. Cover and cook for 10 minutes, until the mussels open. (Discard any that don't open.) Remove the lid and add the green curry puree. Mix well.

While the mussels are cooking, add a 2-count of oil (about 2 tablespoons) to a shallow pan and heat over medium heat. Season flour with salt. Toss shallot slices in seasoned flour to lightly coat; shake off excess. Add shallots to hot pan and fry until crispy. Drain on paper towels. Sprinkle shallots on top of the mussels just before serving. Garnish with lime wedges and cilantro.

CALIFORNIA ARTICHOKES WITH ANCHOVY MAYONNAISE

serves 4 to 6 • time: 40 minutes

Artichokes are natural works of art that require some extra work to prepare and eat but are well worth it. When steamed perfectly, the flesh of the leaves is soft and sweet, not too mushy and not too firm. I love this anchovy mayo for the extra kick it adds to dipping.

1 cup dry white wine
1 quart reduced-sodium chicken broth
4 garlic cloves, peeled
2 bay leaves
2 lemons, halved
4 sprigs fresh thyme
   Extra-virgin olive oil
   Kosher salt and freshly ground black pepper
4 globe artichokes
1 recipe Anchovy Mayonnaise (see recipe, below)

In a large pot heat the wine, broth, garlic, bay leaves, lemons, thyme, and a 2-count of olive oil (about 2 tablespoons) over medium heat; bring to a boil. Season with salt and pepper.

Wash artichokes under cold water. Using a heavy stainless-steel knife, cut off the stems close to the base. Pull off the small, tough lower petals. Place the artichokes in the steaming liquid. Cover and simmer about 30 minutes, until a knife goes into the base of the artichokes without resistance. Drain well. Serve hot or cold with Anchovy Mayonnaise.

ANCHOVY MAYONNAISE Combine 1 garlic clove, peeled; 2 anchovy fillets; 1 cup store-bought mayonnaise; and 2 teaspoons lemon juice in a blender and blend until smooth. Refrigerate until ready to serve.

BAKE

NOTHING IS MORE BEAUTIFUL THAN THE SMELL OF FRESH SOURDOUGH BREAD BAKING AT BOUDIN ON FISHERMAN'S WHARF IN SAN FRANCISCO. I CAN'T GET ENOUGH OF IT.

The baking of fresh breads, cakes, pies, and the like has a special, warm aroma that hits a heartstring every time. And for this reason, historically, great bakers are always some of the most beloved characters in every home, village, town, city, and metropolis the world over. From Granny's fresh apple pies to those incredible cupcakes we line up for on Sunday morning, baking is an art unto itself.

Baking is a lot like roasting in that it involves cooking food in an oven, surrounded by dry heat. And to an extent, you are going for COLOR EQUALS FLAVOR, but far short of that crusty caramelization we would seek on a giant rib roast. In general, baking requires that we cook food at a relatively low temperature for an extended period of time—as opposed to hotter temperatures and faster cooking times for roasting. A great pastry chef—and here's where I really look to define baking—is a stickler for details, temperatures, and particularly measurements. This holds true for home bakers as well. When sautéing, you can freestyle that olive oil into the pan and you'll be okay. But in baking, ¼ teaspoon too much or too little of this or that can throw everything out of whack. Granny bakes your birthday cakes with the steel-eyed precision of a nuclear chemist. And so should you. She's watching. So get out those measuring spoons and let's give Granny a run for her money …

STRAWBERRY-RHUBARB PIE | serves 6 to 8 • time: 1 hour 45 minutes

Rhubarb is an oft-misunderstood vegetable. It is relatively tart and hardly seems at home in a sweet baked pie, however, it adds great dimension when combined with strawberries.

Pastry

3	cups all-purpose flour
¼	cup sugar
	Pinch kosher salt
2	sticks cold unsalted butter, cut into cubes
2	egg yolks
¼	cup ice water

Filling

1½	cups sugar
¾	cup all-purpose flour
¼	teaspoon freshly ground nutmeg
½	teaspoon ground cinnamon
½	stick cold unsalted butter, cut into small cubes
5	cups strawberries, hulled and halved
3	cups finely chopped rhubarb

1	egg
1	tablespoon water
1	tablespoon sugar

Preheat oven to 375°F. To make the pastry, combine the flour, the ¼ cup sugar, and the salt in a food processor and pulse until well combined. Add butter and pulse until the mixture resembles cornmeal. Add the yolks and ice water and pulse again until the dough comes together in a ball. Split the dough in half, wrap in plastic wrap, and refrigerate for 30 minutes.

On a lightly floured surface, roll one ball of dough into a 12-inch circle. Carefully roll the circle around the rolling pin, then unroll it on top of a 10-inch, deep-dish pie plate, gently pressing it around the insides of the dish. Trim excess dough, leaving about ¼ inch of overhang; set aside. Roll the second ball of dough into a 12-inch circle. Cut the circle into 10 strips (for the lattice on the pie). Place dough strips on a tray. Refrigerate dough strips and pie shell while you make the filling.

In a large bowl combine the 1½ cups sugar, the flour, nutmeg, and cinnamon. Fold in butter; stir in strawberries and rhubarb. Pour mixture into pie shell and create a lattice on top with the strips of pastry. Trim excess dough on lattice strips. Fold excess pastry from

the bottom shell up and over the ends of the lattice strips. Pinch edges of pie all the way around. Beat together the egg and water in a small bowl; brush over pie. Sprinkle top with the 1 tablespoon sugar. Place pie plate on a baking sheet and bake about 1 hour and 15 minutes, until crust is golden brown. (Tent the edges with foil if the crust gets too brown.) Cool for 30 minutes before serving.

BUTTERMILK PIE WITH
WHIPPED HONEY CRÈME FRAÎCHE | serves 6 to 8 • time: 2 hours 15 minutes

Below the Mason-Dixon Line, buttermilk pie is a dessert delicacy and it brings back a lot of fond memories of my childhood. Buttermilk is simply milk that has been fermented, much like yogurt. It is thick, rich, and slightly bitter, making beautifully rich custard that, when sweetened a bit, boasts a tantalizing flavor. Golden brown on top and firm yet creamy in the middle, this pie is a true taste of the South that will be a hit anywhere.

Pastry

- 3 cups all-purpose flour
- 2 teaspoons sugar
- 1 teaspoon kosher salt
- 1 stick cold unsalted butter, cut into cubes
- ½ cup vegetable shortening
- ½ cup ice water

Filling

- 1 stick unsalted butter, softened
- 1½ cups sugar
- 3 large eggs, separated
- 2 cups buttermilk
- 1 tablespoon lemon juice
- ¼ teaspoon freshly grated nutmeg
- ¼ cup all-purpose flour

- 1 recipe Honey Crème Fraîche (see recipe, page 195)

To make the pastry, combine flour, the 2 teaspoons sugar, and the salt in a food processor and pulse until well combined. Add butter and shortening and continue to process until the mixture resembles coarse bread crumbs. Add cold water and process until the dough comes together in a large ball. Turn out dough onto a lightly floured surface and gently knead a few times until the dough is smooth. Wrap tightly in plastic wrap and refrigerate for 20 minutes.

Preheat oven to 350°F. On a lightly floured surface, roll the dough into a 12-inch circle. Carefully roll circle of dough around your rolling pin, then unroll it on top of a 10-inch tart pan, gently pressing it around the insides of the pan. Trim any overhang and discard. Cover with a piece of parchment paper and fill with pie weights. Bake in the middle of the preheated oven about 20 minutes or until the crust is set and just firm. Remove weights and cool pie shell.

Reduce the temperature of the oven to 325°F. To make the filling, using the paddle attachment of a kitchen stand mixer bowl beat the butter and the 1½ cups sugar on medium speed until light and fluffy

BELOW THE MASON-DIXON LINE, BUTTERMILK PIE IS A DESSERT DELICACY

and pale in color. Add egg yolks, buttermilk, lemon juice, and nutmeg. Continue to mix until batter is smooth, occasionally scraping down the sides of the bowl with a rubber spatula. Add flour and continue to mix until just combined. Transfer buttermilk mixture to a separate bowl. Thoroughly wash mixing bowl and attachment with soap and hot water; return to stand mixer. Using the whisk attachment, beat egg whites on high until stiff peaks form. Gently fold egg whites, half at a time, into buttermilk mixture. Pour filling into cooled pie shell. Bake for 35 to 40 minutes, until the pie is set (the pie should still be pale in color). Cool. Serve with Honey Crème Fraîche.

HONEY CRÈME FRAÎCHE Using the whisk attachment on a kitchen stand mixer, beat 16 ounces crème fraîche on high for 45 seconds, until it tightens up slightly. Fold in 2 tablespoons honey with a spoon so it is just mixed but you can still see swirls of the honey.

BOURBON AND CHOCOLATE PECAN PIE

serves 6 to 8 • time: 1 hour 20 minutes

Yes, we're heading back down South where bourbon and pecans are a way of life. A good, gooey pecan pie is just about perfect on its own, but add some chocolate and bourbon to the mix to fashion a whole new experience.

Pastry

- 1 cup all-purpose flour, plus more for dusting
- ¼ cup finely ground pecans
- 1 tablespoon sugar
  Pinch kosher salt
- 1 stick cold unsalted butter, cut into cubes
- 2 tablespoons ice water, plus more if needed

Filling

- ½ stick unsalted butter
- 2 ounces unsweetened chocolate
- 3 eggs
- 1 cup sugar
- ¾ cup dark corn syrup or sugar cane syrup (such as Steen's)
- ½ teaspoon pure vanilla extract
- 3 tablespoons bourbon
- ¼ teaspoon kosher salt
- 1½ cups pecan halves

- 1 pint heavy whipping cream, whipped

To make the pastry, in a large bowl combine flour, ground pecans, the 1 tablespoon sugar, and the salt. Add the butter and mix with a pastry blender until the mixture resembles coarse bread crumbs. Sprinkle in the ice water, tossing the mixture with a fork until it is just combined. Squeeze a small amount of dough together; if it is too crumbly, add more ice water, 1 tablespoon at a time. (Do not allow dough to become too wet or sticky.) When dough comes together in a ball, wrap tightly in plastic wrap and refrigerate for at least 30 minutes.

On a lightly floured surface, roll dough into a 12-inch circle. Carefully roll circle of dough around rolling pin, then unroll it on top of a 9-inch pie plate, gently pressing it around the insides of plate. Trim excess dough, leaving ¼ inch overhang. Place the pie pan on a sturdy baking sheet.

Preheat the oven to 350°F. To make the filling, melt the butter and chocolate in a double boiler; remove from heat and let cool. Beat the eggs with an electric mixer on high speed until frothy. Set the mixer on low speed and gradually add the sugar. Stir in the syrup, vanilla, bourbon, salt, and the melted chocolate mixture.

Arrange the pecans on the bottom of the pastry and carefully pour
the egg mixture over them. Bake about 45 minutes, until the filling
is set and slightly puffed. A thin knife stuck in the center of the pie
should come out clean when done. Transfer the pie to rack and cool
completely before cutting. Serve with whipped cream.

THEY ARE AS ELEGANT AS THEY ARE DELICIOUS.

INDIVIDUAL PLUM TARTE
TATIN WITH BLOOD ORANGE CARAMEL

serves 4 • time: 40 minutes

Tarte Tatin is another classic French dessert that is traditionally made with apples and served in slices. With this recipe, I take the same idea and switch the apples with plums. And instead of using a large tart pan, I have created these beauties in individual portions. They are as elegant as they are delicious and will make a perfect finale to your next dinner party.

3 blood oranges, juice only
½ cup sugar, plus 2 tablespoons for sprinkling
1 vanilla bean, split and scraped
½ stick unsalted butter
1 sheet store-bought puff pastry, thawed
4 large plums
2 tablespoons pine nuts
½ cup crème fraîche, to serve

Preheat oven to 400°F. To make the caramel, in a small saucepan heat the blood orange juice, the ½ cup sugar, the vanilla bean and pulp, and the butter over medium heat. Cook and stir for 5 to 7 minutes, until reduced and syrupy. Remove vanilla bean.

Roll out puff pastry sheet on a lightly floured surface and invert a ramekin on top to cut out four circles. Split plums in half and remove stones. Retain four plum halves; cut the other four halves into three wedges each.

Divide the caramel evenly among the four 6-ounce ramekins. Place a plum half, cut-side down, in the caramel, pressing it down firmly. Fill the gaps around the edges using three plum wedges, to form a flat surface. Sprinkle with sugar and top with puff pastry circles. Using the tip of a knife, poke three vents in the top of each to allow steam to escape.

Place ramekins on a baking sheet and bake for 20 to 25 minutes, until the pastry is golden and puffed slightly. Let stand for 15 minutes so the caramel cools slightly. Carefully invert each onto a plate. Top with toasted pine nuts and serve with crème fraîche.

AMARETTO CHOCOLATE BROWNIES | serves 12 • time: 1 hour 10 minutes

There is nothing better than a rich, dense, moist brownie when you are seeking your chocolate fix. But I can't leave it at that. A touch of sweet almond-flavored amaretto makes for a more "adult" brownie—you'll love the results.

- 2 sticks unsalted butter
- 8 ounces bittersweet chocolate chips
- 1¼ cups all-purpose flour
- 1 teaspoon baking powder
  Pinch kosher salt
- 4 large eggs
- 2 cups sugar
- 2 tablespoons amaretto
- 1 recipe Cocoa Whipped Cream (see recipe, below)

Preheat oven to 350°F. Line a 9-inch square baking dish with parchment paper, leaving a 1-inch overhang so you can easily pull brownies out of the pan. Grease parchment paper. Melt butter and chocolate in a double boiler and stir gently until smooth and shiny. Remove from heat to cool slightly.

Sift together flour, baking powder, and salt in a bowl, set aside. Using a kitchen stand mixer, beat eggs, sugar, and amaretto on high speed about 3 minutes, until well combined. Reduce speed to low and slowly pour in melted chocolate mixture, to combine. Gradually add flour mixture and incorporate until just combined.

Transfer batter to prepared baking dish. Bake for 45 to 50 minutes, until a cake tester inserted in the middle comes out clean. Remove from the oven and carefully lift brownie out of dish using the parchment paper ends. Cool brownies; cut into bars. Serve with Cocoa Whipped Cream.

COCOA WHIPPED CREAM Using the whisk attachment on a kitchen stand mixer, beat 1 pint heavy whipping cream, 2 tablespoons cocoa powder, and 2 tablespoons confectioner's sugar on high speed until soft peaks form. Refrigerate until ready to use.

BAKED LIME PUDDING CAKE | serves 4 • time: 1 hour 15 minutes

Here's a favorite of mine that works just as well at home as it does at Bar Florence. Part cake, part pudding, all moist, sweet, and tart goodness. This dessert is just light enough not to slow you down, and the lime is a really refreshing way to wrap up your meal.

1   tablespoon unsalted butter
    Superfine sugar
2   eggs, separated
⅔   cup reduced-fat buttermilk
1   tablespoon lime zest
2   tablespoons lime juice
¼   cup all-purpose flour
⅔   cup superfine sugar
¼   teaspoon kosher salt
    Lime halves and leaves, for garnish

Preheat oven to 325°F. Butter and lightly sugar four 6-ounce ramekins. Using the paddle attachment on a kitchen stand mixer, beat yolks, buttermilk, lime zest, and lime juice on medium speed until well combined. Reduce the speed to low and slowly add flour, the ⅔ cup sugar, and the salt, until just combined. Transfer to another large bowl. Thoroughly wash mixing bowl with soap and hot water; return to stand mixer. Using the whisk attachment, beat egg whites in the clean bowl until stiff peaks form. Gently fold the beaten egg whites into the yolk mixture, a little at a time.

Divide mixture evenly among ramekins. Place ramekins in a roasting pan and fill the pan with hot water halfway up the sides of the ramekins. Bake about 1 hour, until the top springs back when gently pressed and the cakes have a light golden color. Remove ramekins from water; allow to cool slightly. Carefully invert each onto a plate.

BAKING IS AN ART UNTO ITSELF.

BERRY-BRIOCHE BREAD PUDDING WITH LEMON FONDANT

serves 6 to 8 • time: 1 hour

Bread pudding is big in the South, and I have had it a thousand different ways. What I love about this recipe is that it's rich like bread pudding should be, but the berries and the lemon fondant give it a lighter, fresher flavor profile than what's expected. The colorful berries also brighten the presentation, which can otherwise be lacking.

6	eggs, plus 2 egg yolks
¾	cup whole milk
¾	cup heavy whipping cream
¾	cup granulated sugar, plus more for sprinkling
1½	teaspoons pure vanilla extract
½	teaspoon lemon zest
1	12- to 14-ounce loaf brioche
2	cups mixed berries (blueberries, raspberries, blackberries)
1	recipe Lemon Fondant (see recipe, below)

In a large bowl whisk together the eggs and egg yolks, the milk, cream, ¾ cup sugar, vanilla, and lemon zest. Tear the brioche into large pieces; layer with the mixed berries in a deep 9-inch pie dish. Pour the egg mixture over the top and press down gently on top with the flat side of the spoon so the bread soaks up the liquid. Set in the refrigerator for 10 to 15 minutes.

Preheat oven to 350°F. Sprinkle the bread pudding liberally with granulated sugar. Bake in the middle of the oven for 40 to 45 minutes, until pudding has puffed up slightly and the custard is set. (If it gets too brown on the top, tent it with foil while baking.) Serve warm bread pudding with a drizzle of Lemon Fondant.

LEMON FONDANT Thoroughly combine 2 cups confectioner's sugar, the juice of 2 lemons, and 2 teaspoons lemon zest in a bowl. (If necessary, add a splash of water to achieve a drizzling consistency.)

BAKED BREAKFAST APPLES WITH FRENCH TOAST CRUST

serves 6 to 8 • time: 50 minutes

I have been playing around with French toast recipes for as long as I can remember and with this one, I think I've found a keeper. Forget about those drippy slices of white sandwich bread you slap on the griddle. Instead, create this version, a baked masterpiece you will be proud to serve at your next Sunday brunch.

French Toast

3   large eggs
1   cup whole milk
1   teaspoon pure vanilla extract
½   teaspoon ground cinnamon
    Pinch kosher salt
½   12- to 14-ounce loaf challah, cut into 1-inch-thick slices

Filling

½   stick cold unsalted butter, cut into small cubes
½   cup packed light brown sugar
    2 tablespoons dried cranberries
2   tablespoons roughly chopped pecans
½   teaspoon ground cinnamon
6   large Granny Smith apples, peeled, halved, and cored

To prepare the French toast, combine eggs, milk, vanilla, cinnamon, and salt in a shallow bowl; whisk until well combined. Lay challah slices in egg mixture to coat, turning slices occasionally to allow bread to absorb all of the liquid.

For the filling, place a 10-inch oven-safe skillet over medium heat. Add butter and brown sugar and cook for 2 to 3 minutes, until lightly golden and caramelized. Remove from heat. Sprinkle in the cranberries, pecans, and cinnamon. Gently press apple halves into the caramel so they are "standing" and line up one behind another so there is a flat surface on top (you may need to cut some of the halves to fill in the gaps).

Preheat oven to 350°F. Place the soaked slices of challah over apples so they are completely covered. Bake in the middle of the oven for 55 to 60 minutes, until the top is golden and puffy and the apples are knife-tender. Cool slightly. Place a large platter over the top of the skillet. Being very careful, turn the skillet and the platter together, so the skillet is on top and the whole French toast dish comes out on the platter. Remove the skillet. Serve warm.

CRÊPES SUZETTE WITH KUMQUAT-
BUTTER SAUCE AND VANILLA BEAN ICE CREAM

serves 4 to 6 • time: 50 minutes

Crêpes Suzette have been popular in France since the late 1800s, when a 14-year-old waiter purportedly botched a dessert preparation. (Good job!)

Crêpe Batter

2	cups whole milk
2	eggs
1½	cups all-purpose flour
1	stick unsalted butter, melted
	Pinch kosher salt

Kumquat-Butter Sauce

2	sticks unsalted butter
1	cup sugar
1	cup fresh-squeezed orange juice
½	lemon, juice only
1	cup kumquats, sliced
1	vanilla bean, split
1	tablespoon Grand Marnier
1	quart vanilla bean ice cream, to serve

To prepare crêpe batter, place milk and eggs in a blender and blend. Add flour, ½ cup at a time, blending after each addition to ensure a smooth consistency. Add melted butter and salt; blend for 30 seconds until you achieve a smooth, silky consistency. Refrigerate for at least 30 minutes.

For Kumquat-Butter Sauce, in a small saucepan combine the butter, sugar, orange juice, lemon juice, kumquats, and vanilla bean. Cook about 10 minutes, until it just begins to caramelize. Remove pan from heat; add Grand Marnier. Place pan over heat and cook about 10 minutes more until sauce is reduced and syrupy. Set sauce aside and keep warm.

Preheat oven to 350°F. To cook the crêpes, dip a piece of paper towel in vegetable oil and use it to grease a small crepe pan or nonstick skillet. Ladle a spoonful of batter into the pan. Move the pan from side to side, so batter evenly covers the entire bottom. (A good crêpe should be paper-thin.) Cook over high heat; flip crêpe when you see the edge turning golden brown. Remove crêpe from pan and fold in half, then in half again, to form a triangle shape. Repeat with remaining batter. Line up crêpes in a baking dish and spoon sauce over to just cover the crêpes. Bake for 10 to 15 minutes, until crêpes are slightly crispy and brown around the edges and sauce is thick and syrupy. Serve with vanilla bean ice cream.

CARAMEL-COATED POPOVERS | serves 8 to 10 • time: 1 hour

It is generally accepted that popovers are an American derivative of Britain's Yorkshire pudding. I've put my own sweet touch to this version for the ultimate pastry. The egg batter basically "pops" out over the popover tin to make a big, ballooning hollow pastry. Drizzle some sticky delicious caramel over the top and you've made the perfect treat to go with your morning cup of joe.

2 tablespoons unsalted butter
1½ cups all-purpose flour
Pinch kosher salt
1½ cups whole milk, room temperature
3 eggs
2 cups sugar
½ cup water

Preheat oven to 425°F. In a small saucepan melt butter over low heat. Use a small amount of melted butter to grease 12 popover pans; place pans in the oven to heat while you make the batter. Using the whisk attachment of a kitchen stand mixer, beat flour, salt, milk, eggs, and remaining melted butter on high speed for 2 to 3 minutes, until smooth and shiny. Fill the hot popover pans halfway; bake for 30 minutes, until they are puffed and golden.

About 15 minutes before popovers are done baking, prepare caramel. Mix sugar and water in a large saucepan and place over high heat. Cook for 10 to 12 minutes, until sugar melts and the mixture starts to take on a golden brown color. Remove from heat. Working quickly, use two forks to roll the popovers in the caramel and place on parchment paper to set.

GRANNY BAKES YOUR BIRTHDAY CAKES WITH THE STEEL-EYED PRECISION OF A NUCLEAR CHEMIST. AND SO SHOULD YOU.

CARAMELIZED ONION AND ROASTED ROSEMARY FOCACCIA

serves 6 to 8 • time: 2 hours

Savory focaccia is an oven-baked bread that the Italians have been playing with forever. Depending on which region of Italy it hails from, focaccia boasts flavors ranging from olive oil and rosemary to cheese and garlic.

Focaccia Dough

- 2 teaspoons active dry yeast
- 1 cup warm water (heated to 110° to 115°F)
- 2 tablespoons sugar
- 3½ cups all-purpose flour
- 1 teaspoon kosher salt

Topping

- Extra-virgin olive oil
- 2 large onions, sliced
- Kosher salt and freshly ground black pepper
- 4 sprigs fresh rosemary, leaves only
- ¼ cup grated Parmigiano-Reggiano

To prepare the focaccia dough, combine yeast with warm water and sugar in a kitchen stand mixer bowl. Set aside for 5 minutes to dissolve and activate. Using the dough hook attachment, mix the yeast mixture on low speed while slowly adding flour and salt. When all the flour is added, continue kneading the dough on low speed about 10 minutes, until the dough is smooth and elastic. Turn dough onto a lightly floured surface and fold dough over itself a couple of times until smooth. Form the dough into a ball with a smooth surface and place in a greased bowl. Cover with a kitchen towel and set in a warm place for approximately 1 hour, until the dough has doubled in volume.

While the dough is resting, prepare the onion topping. In a large sauté pan heat a 2-count of olive oil (about 2 tablespoons) over medium heat. Add onions; season well with salt and pepper. Cook and stir until onions are golden brown and caramelized.

Preheat oven to 400°F. Grease a baking sheet with oil; turn out dough onto prepared pan. Using your hands, stretch the dough to cover the pan (it should be about ½ inch thick). Cover with a layer of plastic wrap followed by a towel; let stand for 15 minutes.

Uncover the dough and press it down with your fingers in several places to make small dimples. Drizzle lightly with oil and cover with onions, rosemary, and Parmigiano-Reggiano. Season with salt and pepper. Bake for 17 to 20 minutes, until golden. Transfer to a rack to cool.

WHOLE WHEAT PULLMAN LOAF | 1 loaf (about 12 slices) • time: 2 hours 30 minutes

It is said that this loaf took its name from its resemblance to the old Pullman railway cars that used to transport passengers across the United States before we all became prisoners of the interstates. You will recognize the shape as that of traditional sandwich bread, long and rectangular. This whole wheat recipe is hearty, healthy, and absolutely delicious, fresh out of the oven or sliced for tomorrow's sandwich.

2½	teaspoons active dry yeast
1	cup water, warmed (110° to 115°F)
1	cup whole milk
3	cups whole wheat flour
2	cups all-purpose flour
1	tablespoon kosher salt
½	stick butter, room temperature
¼	cup honey
2	tablespoons flaxseeds

In a large bowl combine yeast and warm water. Set aside for 5 minutes to dissolve and activate. Stir milk into yeast mixture. Combine both flours and salt in a kitchen stand mixer bowl. Add butter and, using your fingers, rub it into the flour mixture until the butter is fully incorporated. Make a well in the middle of the flour and add the honey and the milk mixture. Using the dough hook attachment on the mixer, knead the dough about 5 minutes on low speed, until smooth and elastic. Form the dough into a ball and place in a greased bowl. Cover with a kitchen towel and set in a warm place for approximately 1 hour until the dough has doubled in volume.

Turn out dough onto a lightly floured surface. Fold dough over onto itself a couple of times to form a cylinder shape, tucking the ends under so you have a smooth surface on top and the seam underneath the loaf. Place dough in an 8½×4½-inch loaf tin, seam-side down. Cover once more and let rest for 40 to 50 minutes, until it doubles in volume again.

Preheat oven to 400°F. Sprinkle loaf with flaxseeds. Bake loaf about 1 hour, until bread forms a crust and begins to pull away from the sides of the pan. Cool on a wire rack.

PARKER HOUSE ROLLS

serves 8 to 10 • time: 55 minutes *(plus 2 hours resting time)*

This roll was invented over a century ago at the Parker House Hotel in Boston and is still served there today. A lot of history lives inside the Parker House. It's the birthplace of this bread and the Boston Cream Pie as well. And part of its long-standing culinary tradition is the wild and somewhat unbelievable history of employees who have worked their kitchens and dining rooms. This list includes Ho Chi Minh, Malcom X, and Emeril Lagasse. These buttery soft rolls are delicious, and you'll be recreating a bit of history whenever you make them.

3   teaspoons active dry yeast
3   tablespoons warm water (110 to 115°F)
3   tablespoons sugar
1   stick unsalted butter
1   cup whole milk, plus 2 tablespoons for brushing rolls
2   cups bread flour
1   teaspoon kosher salt
2   cups all-purpose flour
1   recipe Garlic-Parsley Butter (see recipe, page 217)

Combine yeast with warm water and the sugar in a kitchen stand mixer bowl. Set aside for 5 minutes to dissolve and activate yeast. In a small saucepan heat 6 tablespoons of the butter and the 1 cup whole milk over low heat; stirring occasionally until butter melts. Add the milk mixture to the yeast. Using the hook attachment on the mixer, fold in the bread flour and salt. Gradually add all-purpose flour to make a dough. (Add only enough all-purpose flour as you need; the dough should come together in a ball that is neither too wet nor too dry.)

Turn out dough onto a lightly floured surface and knead five to six times until dough is smooth and elastic (do not overwork dough or rolls will be tough). Form the dough into a ball and place in a greased bowl. Cover with a kitchen towel and set in a warm place for approximately 1 hour until the dough has doubled in volume.

Butter a 9×5-inch baking dish. Form the dough into 12 to 14 equal-size balls. Arrange the balls in the baking dish so they are in rows just touching one another, then cover with a layer of plastic wrap, then the towel. Set aside to rise again. Once they have doubled in volume again (about 40 minutes), use a pair of kitchen scissors to snip the tops of each bun twice, forming an "X". Set aside for another 15 minutes.

Meanwhile, preheat the oven to 375°F. Using a pastry brush, lightly brush the tops of the rolls with milk. Bake for 20 to 25 minutes, until golden brown. Let the rolls cool in the pan for 2 to 3 minutes before transferring them to a rack. Serve with Garlic-Parsley Butter.

GARLIC-PARSLEY BUTTER Using a wooden spoon, thoroughly combine 2 sticks unsalted butter, room temperature; 2 tablespoons chopped fresh Italian flat-leaf parsley; and 3 cloves garlic, peeled and minced, in a bowl. Season with kosher salt and freshly ground black pepper.

FRESH AND RAW

YEAH, YEAH, I KNOW. COOKING IS TECHNICALLY DEFINED AS THE APPLICATION OF HEAT TO A FOOD PRODUCT. BUT NOT EVERYTHING I MAKE INVOLVES HEAT.

Sometimes, the best ingredients in a time and place are just fine the way they are. Cool, crisp, raw, and fresh. No, I'm not asking you to get out your sashimi knife just yet, but raw ingredients can be important components of a meal unto themselves.

On a lot of plates, in restaurants or at home, you will find both cooked and raw ingredients working in harmony. Sometimes they work together. Sometimes they work side by side. What I'm looking to show you here is how the balance between the two can make all the difference in what you are trying to get across with your dish. On a hot summer day, I love nothing more than a fresh, crisp salad with vibrant greens and a bright citrus vinaigrette. It will cool you off and give you just what you need to survive the heat. If you want to beef it up a bit (pardon the pun) with some protein or add in a cooked component for warmth or texture, go for it. But at the end of the day, the dish is built on a foundation of raw, fresh ingredients that dictate its character. Typically, when dealing with raw and fresh ingredients, you're going to want to pay special attention to how you dress them. Give them some flavor that can change according to your mood. Let's learn a few basics that can take us in a bunch of directions.

Think fresh, think raw, and let's get cooking … kinda …

FRESH & RAW

clean greens

I EAT A LOT OF SALADS. LIGHT, FRESH SUMMER SALADS. HEARTY, WARM SALADS. MEAL-SIZE SALADS CHOCK-FULL OF PROTEIN.

But whatever kind of salad I'm wanting, the preparation usually starts with a bunch of greens that I have brought home from the market. And as hungry as I may be, I know that the first step to building a beautiful salad is giving my greens the proper attention to leave them clean, crisp, and gorgeous.

Let's remember that these lettuces came out of the ground at some point, so we have to clean them to make them edible. You always have the option of picking up a bag of the prewashed stuff at the supermarket but I don't recommend it. The greens may indeed be clean and you'll save a bit of time but keep in mind that they have been bagged for some time and aren't nearly as fresh. I always buy fresh heads of lettuce and take a few extra minutes to prepare them.

To clean your lettuce properly, start by cutting or breaking off the root and separating the leaves. Then grab a large bowl, fill it with ice water and place the leaves gently into the water. After about 30 seconds, the dirt and sand will fall off the leaves and sink to the bottom of the bowl. Pull the leaves out, shake them gently, and blot them dry with a clean dish towel or paper towel. Or if you have a salad spinner, give it spin for cleaning and drying your greens. To store your freshly cleaned leaves, simply wrap them in paper towels, place them in a plastic bag, and pop them in the fridge. They'll last about a week in the fridge and will outlive that prewashed grocery store stuff every time.

Simple, right? Follow these steps and you're off to a great start for the best, freshest salads of your life.

CAESAR SALAD | serves 4 • time: 15 minutes

Here is the perfect opportunity to use the new lettuce cleaning technique I detailed in the chapter intro (see page 220). Keep your lettuce clean and crisp by soaking it in an ice water bath and you're off to a good start. Making a proper Caesar dressing is truly an art form and is very subjective. Check out my version and let me know what you think.

- 4 anchovy fillets
- 2 egg yolks
- 1 tablespoon Dijon mustard
- 2 lemons, juice only
- 2 tablespoons water
- ½ cup extra-virgin olive oil
- ¼ cup freshly grated Parmigiano-Reggiano, plus extra for garnish
   Kosher salt and freshly ground black pepper

- 1 clove garlic, peeled and smashed with a pinch of salt and a little extra-virgin olive oil
- 2 heads romaine lettuce
- 1 bunch fresh hydroponic watercress
- ¼ French baguette, thinly sliced and toasted

In a blender combine the anchovies, yolks, mustard, lemon juice, and water and process for 30 seconds, until smooth. With the blender running, slowly pour in the oil. Stir in the Parmigiano-Reggiano, a pinch of salt, and some pepper. Refrigerate the dressing until ready to use.

To assemble the salad, smear the garlic paste over the inside of a large salad bowl. Tear the lettuce into the salad bowl. Add watercress and toss together. Add enough dressing to coat the salad as desired. Garnish with some additional cheese. Toss the salad well and serve immediately with toasted baguette slices.

CALIFORNIA COBB WITH POACHED
SHRIMP AND GREEN GODDESS DRESSING

serves 4 • time: 30 minutes

You have seen this salad before, but I swear, this is the best version you'll ever eat. The creamy green dressing looks amazing and adds an herby twist to the classic recipe. The Cobb salad is inherently Californian in that it was invented in Los Angeles. I have loaded it with some of the best local ingredients I can find to up the California factor even more. Thick bacon, creamy blue cheese, juicy tomatoes, and fresh shrimp put this salad over the top.

Green Goddess Dressing

- ½ cup sour cream
- ½ cup store-bought mayonnaise
- 1 lemon, juice only
- 2 garlic cloves, peeled and roughly chopped
- 1 anchovy fillet
- ½ cup roughly chopped fresh Italian flat-leaf parsley
- ¼ cup roughly chopped fresh cilantro
- 2 tablespoons chopped fresh tarragon
- 2 tablespoons chopped fresh chives
  Water, as needed
  Kosher salt and freshly ground black pepper

Shrimp

- 1 lemon, halved
- 1 bay leaf
- 4 sprigs fresh thyme
- 4 black peppercorns
- 2 garlic cloves, peeled
- 1 tablespoon kosher salt
- 24 large shrimp, peeled and deveined

- 2 heads Bibb lettuce, leaves torn into bite-size pieces
- 8 slices bacon, cooked and cut into pieces
- ⅔ cup medium-size black pitted olives
- 1 cup grape tomatoes, halved
- 1 cup crumbled blue cheese
- 4 eggs, hard-boiled and halved lengthwise
- 4 sprigs fresh cilantro, for garnish

To make the Green Goddess Dressing, combine sour cream, mayonnaise, lemon juice, garlic, anchovy, and herbs in a blender and puree until light green and creamy. Add water as needed to achieve a smooth, light consistency. Cover with plastic wrap and set aside in the refrigerator to allow the flavors to come together. When ready to use, add additional lemon juice and season with salt and pepper.

Fill a large pot with about ½ gallon water. Squeeze in the lemon juice and toss in lemon halves for extra flavor. Add the bay leaf, thyme, peppercorns, garlic, and salt. Bring to a boil over medium heat. Simmer for 5 minutes to infuse the water with the aromatics. Before adding shrimp, bring water to a rolling boil. Add the shrimp, then remove from heat and allow shrimp to poach for 7 to 8 minutes, until they turn pink. Using a slotted spoon, transfer the shrimp from the poaching liquid to a bowl. Chill shrimp in refrigerator.

To assemble, combine the lettuce, bacon, olives, grape tomatoes, and blue cheese in a bowl. Toss with Green Goddess Dressing to coat evenly. Arrange egg on top, followed by poached shrimp. Sprinkle with blue cheese. Garnish with cilantro.

POACHED SHRIMP AND WATERCRESS SALAD | serves 2 to 4 • time: 35 minutes

This delicate yet satisfying salad lets the natural sweetness of shrimp shine against the slightly peppery and bitter watercress. It looks elegant on the plate and sophisticated enough to serve anytime.

Shrimp
2   teaspoons sea salt
2   lemons, halved, plus more for serving
3   bay leaves
8   sprigs fresh thyme
1   tablespoon Old Bay seasoning
2   pounds jumbo shrimp, with shells, heads, and tails on

Salad
1   ruby grapefruit
1   bunch fresh hydroponic watercress or other peppery green
¼   cup crumbled blue cheese
    Extra-virgin olive oil
    Kosher salt and freshly ground black pepper
2   tablespoons slivered almonds, toasted

Fill a large pot with about ½ gallon water. Add the sea salt, squeeze in the lemon juice, and toss in the lemon halves for extra flavor. Add the bay leaves, thyme, and Old Bay seasoning. Bring to a boil over medium heat. Simmer for 5 minutes to infuse the water with the aromatics. Add the shrimp, bring back to a simmer, then remove from heat to allow shrimp to poach about 7 to 8 minutes, until they turn pink. Using a slotted spoon, transfer the shrimp to a bowl. Chill thoroughly in the refrigerator before peeling.

For the salad, set the grapefruit on a cutting board and use a knife to cut off all of the peel, removing as much of the white pith as you can. Use a small knife to carefully cut between membranes, releasing the sections. Combine grapefruit sections and watercress on a platter. Scatter crumbled blue cheese over the top and drizzle with oil. Sprinkle with salt and pepper. Sprinkle the almonds over the top, add poached shrimp, and serve.

WEST COAST DUNGENESS CRAB AND
ASPARAGUS SALAD WITH LEMONY HOLLANDAISE | serves 4 to 6 • time: 45 minutes

You haven't had a crab until you have tried the fresh Dungeness from San Francisco Bay. Sweet lump crabmeat is a true delicacy. Here, it works perfectly with asparagus and rich hollandaise, which I've brightened up with extra lemon.

1 bunch asparagus (about 1 pound)
2 shallots, thinly sliced
½ cup all-purpose flour
   Kosher salt and freshly ground black pepper
   Vegetable oil, for frying
2 pounds lump crabmeat, picked over to remove shells and cartilage

Hollandaise Sauce
2 egg yolks
1 teaspoon dry mustard
   Pinch cayenne pepper
2 tablespoons water
2 sticks unsalted butter, melted
1 lemon, juice only
   Kosher salt and freshly ground black pepper

8 sprigs fresh tarragon, for garnish

Trim the woody ends of the asparagus; discard. Lightly peel about an inch from the base of asparagus to remove tougher outer skin. Prepare a large bowl of ice water. Bring a pot of salted water to a boil. Add the asparagus and cook for 2 to 3 minutes, until tender. Remove the asparagus and plunge in ice water. Leave the asparagus in the water for 2 minutes, until chilled (to stop the cooking process). Drain and pat dry with paper towels.

Separate the shallot slices into rings. Season flour with salt and black pepper. Dredge shallots in seasoned flour, shaking off excess. Heat ¼ inch oil in an small skillet over medium-high heat. Fry shallots until crispy and golden. Drain on paper towels and season with salt and black pepper; set aside. Drain crabmeat and remove excess moisture with paper towels if necessary.

To make the hollandaise sauce, combine egg yolks, mustard, cayenne, and water in a blender. Blend until combined, then with the motor running, slowly pour in the melted butter. Stop blending when all the butter has been incorporated. Season to taste with lemon juice, salt, and black pepper. (Thin sauce with water if it is too thick.)

Serve a generous spoonful of crabmeat on top of asparagus. Drizzle with hollandaise, sprinkle with shallots, and garnish with tarragon.

BRUSSELS SPROUTS SALAD
WITH PANCETTA AND CRANBERRIES | serves 4 to 6 • time: 30 minutes

It's not easy to get Brussels sprouts into your kids' diet, but the crispy pancetta and the sweet tart cranberries are the perfect complements to the browned leaves of the sprouts. And by separating the leaves, you might even get these sprouts past the most suspicious kids.

2 pounds baby Brussels sprouts
Extra-virgin olive oil
6 ounces pancetta, cut into small dice (1½ cups)
¼ cup dried cranberries
3 tablespoons shallots, finely chopped
1 garlic clove, peeled and minced
2 tablespoons balsamic vinegar
¼ cup chicken broth
Kosher salt and freshly ground black pepper

Pick all the Brussels sprouts apart so you have one big pile of leaves. In a large sauté pan heat a 2-count of olive oil (about 2 tablespoons) over medium heat. Add the pancetta and cook for 2 to 3 minutes, until the fat renders and the pancetta is crispy. Add the separated Brussels sprouts leaves, cranberries, shallots, and garlic. Toss well to combine all the ingredients. Add the balsamic vinegar and chicken broth and continue to cook for 3 to 4 minutes, until the Brussels sprouts leaves have just wilted. Season to taste with salt and pepper. Serve warm.

I THINK EVEN YOUR KIDS WILL EAT THIS ONE!

NOT EVERY SALAD INSPIRED BY THE FLAVORS OF THE FAR EAST IS BUILT ON A FOUNDATION OF CANNED MANDARIN ORANGES.

CRISPY ASIAN CHICKEN SALAD | serves 2 to 4 • time: 25 minutes

Believe it or not, not every salad inspired by the flavors of the Far East is built on a foundation of canned mandarin oranges. Explore the Asian influence of honey-sesame-glazed chicken and rice wine vinaigrette for a new and exciting take on this meal-size salad.

Glaze

1   ½-inch piece ginger, peeled and grated
1   tablespoon toasted sesame seeds
1   tablespoon toasted sesame oil
1   tablespoon honey
2   tablespoons reduced-sodium soy sauce

   Extra-virgin olive oil
1   large boneless chicken breast (skin on), halved
   Kosher salt and freshly ground black pepper

1   zucchini, sliced lengthwise
6   wonton wrappers, cut into strips, deep-fried, and salted
¼   bunch fresh cilantro, for garnish

Preheat oven to 375°F. For the glaze, combine the ginger, sesame seeds, sesame oil, honey, and soy sauce in a small bowl and stir to mix. Set aside.

In a large sauté pan heat a 2-count of olive oil (about 2 tablespoons) over medium heat. Season the chicken on both sides with salt and pepper. Place the breasts, skin sides down, in the pan and sear for 3 to 5 minutes, until golden. Turn the breasts over and, using a pastry brush, liberally brush the glaze on top of the skin. Place the whole pan in the preheated oven and roast for 7 to 10 minutes, until chicken juices run clear (180°F). Baste with glaze throughout cooking so the breast remains moist and tender. Let chicken stand until ready to serve the salad, then slice chicken.

Arrange zucchini strips on the bottom of a plate and top with sliced chicken breast. Scatter crispy wonton strips on top and drizzle with pan juices. Garnish with cilantro.

HEIRLOOM TOMATOES AND BLACK-EYED PEAS | serves 4 to 6 • time: 15 minutes

You can throw this salad together quickly for a healthy yet hearty combination of textures and flavors. Select your tomatoes according to the season, but I definitely recommend using heirlooms if they're available. The black-eyed peas are a nod to my Southern roots. Add the watercress, and you have a substantial salad that's a great choice for your vegetarian friends.

6   large ripe heirloom tomatoes, various colors and varieties
2   cups canned black-eyed peas, cooked
½   small red onion
1   tablespoon red wine vinegar
¼   cup extra-virgin olive oil
    Kosher salt and freshly ground black pepper
¼   bunch fresh hydroponic watercress, for garnish

Cut tomatoes into thick slices and lay them on a large plate in a single layer, mixing the colors and varieties. Drain black-eyed peas and rinse under cold water. Scatter black-eyed peas over tomatoes. Using a sharp knife, cut the red onion in half lengthwise (root to tip). Slice each onion half lengthwise to create thin crescent-shape slices. Scatter onion on top of black-eyed peas.

In a small bowl whisk together vinegar and oil; drizzle over salad and season with salt and pepper. Garnish with watercress.

I DEFINITELY
RECOMMEND
USING
HEIRLOOMS
IF THEY'RE
AVAILABLE.

ARUGULA, FENNEL, AND GRAPE SALAD | serves 4 • time: 10 minutes

I just love the combination of peppery arugula with the slightly sweet licorice flavor of fennel. Throw in bright, juicy grapes and crunchy cashews, and you have a flavorful salad that is as interesting to look at as it is to eat.

- 2 tablespoons lemon juice
- 1 teaspoon Dijon mustard
- ½ cup extra-virgin olive oil
- 2 teaspoons sugar
  Kosher salt and freshly ground black pepper
- 1 small fennel bulb
- 4 cups packed baby arugula
- 1 cup red seedless grapes
- ½ cup roasted cashews

To prepare vinaigrette, combine lemon juice and mustard in a large bowl. Slowly pour in the oil, whisking until the mixture has emulsified. Season with sugar, about ½ teaspoon salt, and black pepper.

Wash fennel bulb. Using a mandoline or sharp knife, shave the fennel lengthwise so each piece is still held together by the root. Drop shaved fennel pieces in a large bowl of ice water for 1 minute to crisp; drain and dry.

When ready to serve, toss fennel, arugula, grapes, and cashews together in a large salad bowl. Toss salad with the vinaigrette, to coat. Season to taste with salt and pepper.

SOMETIMES, THE BEST INGREDIENTS IN A TIME AND PLACE ARE JUST FINE THE WAY THEY ARE.

CALIFORNIA PEACH, SHAVED FENNEL, MOZZARELLA, AND CRISPY PROSCIUTTO SALAD

serves 4 to 6 • time: 14 minutes

I put this salad together for one of the first dinner parties I had at my new house, and it was a hit from the get-go. The creamy, fresh mozzarella really highlights the salty, crunchy bits of prosciutto and the sweet, juicy flesh of the peaches. This is one that nobody will see coming.

8   thin slices prosciutto (about ⅓ pound)
4   peaches, firm but ripe, halved and pitted
½   fennel bulb
2   balls (8 ounces each) fresh buffalo mozzarella,
      cut into bite-size pieces
2   cups fresh hydroponic watercress or other peppery green
2   tablespoons balsamic vinegar
¼   cup extra-virgin olive oil
     Kosher salt and freshly ground black pepper

Preheat oven to 350°F. Lay prosciutto slices out flat in a single layer on a baking tray. Bake for 15 to 20 minutes, until crispy and golden. Remove from tray and drain on paper towels.

Cut peaches into thick wedges; set aside. Using a mandoline or sharp knife, shave fennel into paper-thin crescents. Drop fennel slices in a large bowl of ice water for 1 minute to crisp; drain and dry on paper towels. Toss peaches, fennel, mozzarella, and watercress together in a large salad bowl.

To prepare the dressing, put balsamic vinegar in a small bowl. Whisking constantly, slowly pour in oil until mixture emulsifies slightly. Season with salt and pepper. Drizzle individual servings of salad with dressing; top with crispy prosciutto.

CRUNCHY JICAMA, MANGO, AND CUCUMBER SALAD

serves 4 to 6 • time: 20 minutes

It doesn't get any lighter, brighter, or fresher than this crispy salad, inspired by the roadside stands in Mexico. The sweetness of the mango and the coolness of the cucumber and the jicama are a great counter to the tart heat of the lime and chile vinaigrette. Dish this up on a hot summer day, and you're in business.

- 1   medium jicama (about 1 pound)
- 2   small cucumbers
- 3   medium mangoes
- 4   radishes, rinsed
- 4   sprigs fresh cilantro, leaves only
- 1   teaspoon chopped red chile (or to taste)
- 2   limes, juice only
     Extra-virgin olive oil
     Kosher salt
     Fresh cilantro, for garnish

Peel and cut the jicama into 2-inch-long wedges (the size of a large oven fry). Slice the cucumbers in half, scoop out the seeds, then cut into wedges so similar in size to the jicama. Peel the mangoes and cut the cheeks off. Slice into wedges. Using a mandoline or a sharp knife, finely slice radishes.

Combine jicama, cucumbers, mangoes, radishes, cilantro, dried red chile flakes, and lime juice in a large bowl. Drizzle with a little oil and toss well to coat. When ready to serve, season with a little salt and garnish with cilantro.

IT DOESN'T GET ANY LIGHTER, BRIGHTER, OR FRESHER THAN THIS.

FRISÉE WITH PEARS, GOAT CHEESE, AND SALTED PECANS

serves 4 • prep time: 20 minutes

I love fruit in salads, and in the middle of winter, these sweet, juicy pears are a nice treat. Match them with rich goat cheese and toasted pecans, and you have some really interesting textures going on.

Dressing

1 cup crème fraîche
2 tablespoons Dijon mustard
½ lemon, juice only
1 tablespoon sugar
1 shallot, minced
   Kosher salt and freshly ground black pepper

Salad

2 medium ripe Bosc pears
8 cups frisée lettuce
¾ cup pecan halves, toasted
¾ cup crumbled goat cheese

In a small bowl combine crème fraîche, mustard, lemon juice, and sugar. Fold in shallot and season with salt and pepper. Cover and set aside in refrigerator to let the flavors come together.

Meanwhile, for the salad, halve, core, and cut the pears into thin slices. Toss pear slices together with frisée leaves and toasted pecans in a large salad bowl. Drizzle with dressing and fold in the crumbled goat cheese. Serve immediately.

IN THE MIDDLE OF WINTER, THESE SWEET, JUICY PEARS, ARE A NICE TREAT.

ENDIVE, ORANGE, AND RADICCHIO | serves 4 to 6 • time: 15 minutes

Tangy and bitter endive, sweet and sour orange rounds, and a rich and creamy dressing make a combination you don't normally find. The colors on this one really pop, and I love the way the acid of the oranges meets the crème fraîche.

Dressing
- 1 cup crème fraîche
- 2 tablespoons Dijon mustard
- ½ lemon, juice only
- 1 tablespoon sugar
- 1 shallot, minced
- Kosher salt and freshly ground black pepper

Salad
- 2 heads endive, leaves separated
- 2 heads baby radicchio, leaves torn into large pieces
- 1 orange, peeled and cut into slices through the equator (horizontally)
- 1 blood orange, peeled and cut into slices through the equator (horizontally)

For the dressing, in a small bowl combine crème fraîche, mustard, lemon juice, and sugar. Fold in shallot and season with salt and pepper. Cover and set aside in refrigerator to let the flavors come together.

For the salad, toss together the endive, radicchio, and both types of orange slices in a large salad bowl. Drizzle with dressing and gently toss to coat. Taste and adjust seasoning. Serve immediately.

ON A HOT SUMMER DAY, I LOVE NOTHING MORE THAN A FRESH, CRISP SALAD.

ZUCCHINI RICOTTA BRUSCHETTA serves 4 to 6 • time: 35 minutes

Next time you are thinking about throwing together some bruschetta, try something new and fresh with this zucchini carpaccio. A tangy marinade with cilantro, tarragon, and mint gives the beautifully thin ribbons of squash a bright zest that really shines against the creamy ricotta. All of this on top of the crunchy grilled bread … yum.

1   zucchini
    Kosher salt
2   tablespoons chopped fresh mint leaves
    Extra-virgin olive oil
    Freshly ground black pepper
½   French baguette
1   garlic clove, peeled and halved lengthwise
2   cups whole-milk ricotta
1   teaspoon Meyer lemon zest

Using a mandoline or sharp knife, shave zucchini lengthwise into paper-thin ribbons. Lay ribbons flat in a single layer on a kitchen towel and sprinkle liberally with salt. Let stand for 10 minutes until the salt has drawn some of the water out of the zucchini and ribbons are pliable. Wash zucchini ribbons under cold running water, drain, and pat dry with paper towels. Toss ribbons with fresh mint and drizzle with oil. Season with salt and pepper.

Preheat oven 350°F. Cut baguette into ¾-inch slices of the baguette on a bias. Lay bread slices on a roasting tray and drizzle with oil. Bake until golden brown on both sides, turning once. Remove from oven and rub with garlic while still warm.

In a medium bowl combine ricotta and lemon zest; season with salt and pepper. Stir until well combined and the ricotta is light and fluffy.

To assemble bruschetta, heap a small spoonful of ricotta mix on each piece of toasted bread. Top with a few layered slices zucchini and mint. Finish with a sprinkle of salt on top.

One cannot think well,
love well, sleep well, if one has
not dined well.
~Virginia Woolf

THANKS

THIS BOOK WAS SUCH AN INTERESTING AND EXCITING JOURNEY AND THERE ARE MANY PEOPLE TO THANK.

My deepest appreciation to:

My photographer, Squire Fox, and his assistant, David Sullivan—you outdid yourselves and the photos are beyond what I ever imagined.

John Lee, for the outstanding cover shot and chapter openers—you are a great guy and have such an eye.

The entire team of food stylists and assistants masterfully led by Kevin Crafts—Victoria, Rochelle, Penny, and Wes. Thank you for the long hours and impeccable work.

My Florence Group team—Sarah Esterling, Reid Strathearn, Anthony Hoy Fong, John Mucci, Diane Melkonian, Rick Eisenberg, Robyn West, and Joe Conforti. Without all of your hard work and dedication, this operation wouldn't run like the well-oiled machine it is. Thank you for doing it everyday.

My family and friends at the Food Network, especially my friend Mark Dissin and the crew of "Tyler's Ultimate". Getting together with you every few months and banging out a new season of shows is always inspiring. I am lucky to work with such a top-notch team.

Our dear friends who taste and sample anything new and exciting that I dream up—the good and the bad: Jen Andrews, Laura Hiser, Jerry Pennacoli, Adam Durtiz, Max and Jillian, Andrei, Nikki and The DeBartolo Family, The Lelands, Kai Mathey, Lee Schrager, The Pikeys, and Dr. Wilner. Our interesting and cool Mill Valley neighbors: Nina, Chris and Holden, Casey, Mike and Vegas, Deborah and Jonathan, Matt and Kara, Sammy and Kari, Tiffanie and Scott, and Andrew and Meagan. And Peter and Robert at my favorite local restaurants—The Buckeye and Bungalow 44—thanks for all of the homemade meals to go and such memorable family meals.

My parents Dad and Jan, Mom and John, Warren, Michael, Ryan, the Pace Family, and my in-laws: Larry "Frank" Moss, Marjorie Clark, Cavan, Jordan, Doug. Also our extended family: Janet and Chuck, BG, Nick and Dick, and Esperanza and Hilda. And a moment to mention the grandmothers we lost last year: Dorothy "Dodie" Krahl and Emily Wilson. We all miss you.

Finally, a special thank you to my lovely wife Tolan who has somehow managed to keep up with the hectic pace of my life, all while pregnant with two children back to back. Here is to our beautiful family and our house full of wonderful children: Miles, Hayden, and Dorothy.

I would also like to thank Viking, the Gene Schick Company, Heath Ceramics, Wüsthof, LamsonSharp Knives, All-Clad cookware, Mauviel cookware, Ruffoni Italian copper cookware, Falk, Proteak cutting boards from sustainable forests, Anchor Hocking, Golden Gate Meat Company, Cowgirl Creamery, Hog Island Oyster Company, Fish in Sausalito, Whole Foods, McEvoy olive oil, Mikasa, Dean & DeLuca, Ozark West, Shun, Outset, Crushpad, and The Mill Valley Market for all of their help with the book.

CREATE A PERFECT MEAL WITH TYLER FLORENCE
DINNER AT MY PLACE

> A PEEK INTO LIFE AT HOME WITH TYLER.

> THE BOOK IS ORGANIZED BY OCCASION, SUCH AS HIS WIFE'S BIRTHDAY PARTY, SUNDAY NIGHT DINNER BY THE FIRE AND GAME NIGHT WITH THE GUYS.

> MENUS AND PERSONAL PHOTOS FROM TYLER'S HOME-COOKED MEALS AND DINNER PARTIES.

AVAILABLE
WHERE ALL
GREAT BOOKS
ARE SOLD!

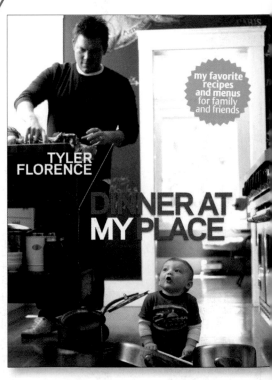

my favorite recipes and menus for family and friends

TYLER FLORENCE

DINNER AT MY PLACE